T0303287

HSOAC
HOMELAND SECURITY
OPERATIONAL ANALYSIS CENTER

Modeling the Impact of Border-Enforcement Measures

ELINA TREYGER, MICHAEL ROBBINS, JOSEPH C. CHANG, STEPHANIE TANVERAKUL

Published in 2020

Preface

This report presents the results of a project conducted under the title "Human Migration Modeling." The goal of this project was to explore the use of statistical modeling methods to estimate the effects of border-enforcement measures—such as technology, infrastructure, and personnel—on outcomes relevant to border security. As a result of consultations with stakeholders within U.S. Customs and Border Protection, the project focused on a subset of stationary surveillance technology, investigating the effects of the deployment of such technology assets on U.S. Border Patrol apprehensions of unlawful migrants between ports of entry along the southwest border. The project employed quasi-experimental statistical methods that are commonly used in social-science research to evaluate the effects of various interventions (such as policy changes).

This report presents the results of our analysis and the lessons we extracted from it for the broader goal of assessing the potential that statistical modeling holds for improving the evidence base relevant to border-enforcement policies and operations. Through the reported analysis and its implications, we aspired to advance the understanding of the impact or effectiveness of border-enforcement measures. The report should be of interest to both operational commanders and policymakers within the U.S. Department of Homeland Security (DHS), particularly within Customs and Border Protection. The report demonstrates a mode of analysis that yields evidence relevant to investment decisions, operational decisions, and planning within DHS. It should also be of interest to other policy and academic researchers, as well as the broader community of experts engaged in immigration enforcement and border security policy.

This research was sponsored by DHS's Science and Technology Directorate and conducted within the Strategy, Policy, and Operations Program of the Homeland Security Operational Analysis Center (HSOAC) federally funded research and development center (FFRDC).

About the Homeland Security Operational Analysis Center

The Homeland Security Act of 2002 (Section 305 of Public Law 107-296, as codified at 6 U.S.C. § 185) authorizes the Secretary of Homeland Security, acting through the Under Secretary for Science and Technology, to establish one or more FFRDCs to provide independent analysis of homeland security issues. The RAND Corporation operates HSOAC as an FFRDC for DHS under contract HSHQDC-16-D-00007.

The HSOAC FFRDC provides the government with independent and objective analyses and advice in core areas important to the department in support of policy development, decisionmaking, alternative approaches, and new ideas on issues of significance. The HSOAC FFRDC also works with and supports other federal, state, local, tribal, and public- and private-sector organizations that make up the homeland security enterprise. The HSOAC FFRDC's research is undertaken by mutual consent with DHS and is organized as a set of discrete tasks. This report presents the results of research and analysis conducted under task 70RSAT18FR0000142, Human Migration Modeling.

The results presented in this report do not necessarily reflect official DHS opinion or policy.

For more information on HSOAC, see www.rand.org/hsoac. For more information on this publication, see www.rand.org/t/RR4348.

Contents

Preface ... iii
Figures ... vii
Tables ... ix
Summary ... xi
Acknowledgments ... xvii
Abbreviations ... xix

CHAPTER ONE
Introduction: Studying the Effects of Border-Enforcement Measures ... 1
Policy Background ... 2
Study Scope: Surveillance Technology Between Ports of Entry ... 3
The Challenge of Evaluating the Effectiveness or Impact of Border-Enforcement Measures ... 5
The Expected Effects of Surveillance Technology ... 11

CHAPTER TWO
Methodology: Identifying the Effects of Surveillance Technology, Using Statistical Methods for Causal Inference ... 15
Difference-in-Differences Design ... 16
Synthetic Control Methods ... 17
Synthesizing Multiple Methods ... 18

CHAPTER THREE
What Do Data and Statistical Analysis Tell Us? ... 21
Describing the Data ... 21
Findings and Discussion ... 28

CHAPTER FOUR
The Path Forward and Conclusions: Implications for the Department of Homeland Security ... 45
Limitations of Quasi-Experimental Methods and the Available Data ... 45

The Promise and Possibilities of Quasi-Experimental Methods.................................47
Concluding Observations: Implications for the Department of Homeland Security........ 50

APPENDIX
Technical Details..53

Bibliography..65

Figures

3.1. Border Patrol Zones That Touch the U.S.–Mexico Border........................ 23
3.2. Monthly Total U.S. Border Patrol Apprehensions, by Sector, 2008–2019....... 24
3.3. Monthly U.S. Border Patrol Apprehensions of Migrants from Mexico, by Sector, 2008–2019...25
3.4. Monthly U.S. Border Patrol Apprehensions of Migrants from Central America, by Sector, 2008–2019...25
3.5. Number of Zones Treated by Integrated Fixed Tower, Tactical Aerostat System, Rapid Aerostat Initial Deployment Tower, and Remote Video Surveillance System Technologies, by Month....................................... 26
3.6. Apprehension Levels in the Months Before and After Deployment of Integrated Fixed Towers, by Zone.. 27
3.7. Apprehension Levels in the Months Before and After Deployment of Tactical Aerostat Systems and Rapid Aerostat Initial Deployment Towers, by Zone.. 28
3.8. Apprehension Levels in the Months Before and After Deployment of Remote Video Surveillance System Towers, by Zone................................29
3.9. Difference-in-Differences Regression Results, Basic Model........................32
3.10. Difference-in-Differences Regression Results, Divergent-Trends Model..........33
3.11. Difference-in-Differences Regression Results, Sector-Specific Models in the Tucson and Rio Grande Valley Sectors..35
3.12. Synthetic Control Method Results: Comparing Apprehension Trends in Zones Treated with Integrated Fixed Towers and Synthetic Control Zones.....37
3.13. Synthetic Control Method Results: Comparing Apprehension Trends in Zones Treated with Tactical Aerostat Systems and Synthetic Control Zones... 38
3.14. Synthetic Control Method Results: Comparing Apprehension Trends in Zones Treated with Rapid Aerostat Initial Deployment Towers and Synthetic Control Zones..39
3.15. Synthetic Control Method Results: Comparing Apprehension Trends in Zones Treated with Remote Video Surveillance Systems and Synthetic Control Zones.. 40

Tables

S.1. Summary of Findings Across Models, with Qualitative Assessments of the Strength of Evidence ... xiv
1.1. Expected Effects of Surveillance Technology on Unobserved and Observed Metrics ... 12
3.1. Difference-in-Differences Model Summary ... 30
3.2. Summary of Findings Across Models, with Qualitative Assessments of the Strength of Evidence ... 40
A.1. Difference-in-Differences Regression Results, Basic Models, Separate ... 55
A.2. Difference-in-Differences Regression Results, Basic Models, Joint ... 55
A.3. Difference-in-Differences Regression Results, Divergent-Trends Models, Joint ... 56
A.4. Difference-in-Differences Regression Results, Divergent-Trends Models, Separate ... 56
A.5. Difference-in-Differences Regression Results, Sector-Specific Models ... 56
A.6. Synthetic Control Method Results for Integrated Fixed Tower Deployment in Region 1: Five Zones in August 2015 ... 59
A.7. Synthetic Control Method Results for Integrated Fixed Tower Deployment in Region 2: Seven Zones in April 2017 ... 59
A.8. Synthetic Control Method Results for Integrated Fixed Tower Deployment in Region 3: Six Zones in October 2017 ... 59
A.9. Synthetic Control Method Results for Integrated Fixed Tower Deployment in Region 4: Five Zones in September 2018 ... 60
A.10. Synthetic Control Method Results for Integrated Fixed Tower Deployment in Region 5: Four Zones in December 2018 ... 60
A.11. Synthetic Control Method Results for Tactical Aerostat System Deployment in Region 1: Six Zones in January 2014 ... 60
A.12. Synthetic Control Method Results for Tactical Aerostat System Deployment in Region 2: Ten Zones in August 2015 ... 61
A.13. Synthetic Control Method Results for Rapid Aerostat Initial Deployment Tower Deployment in Region 1: Two Zones in October 2015 ... 61
A.14. Synthetic Control Method Results for Rapid Aerostat Initial Deployment Tower Deployment in Region 2: Two Zones in November 2015 ... 61

A.15. Synthetic Control Method Results for Rapid Aerostat Initial Deployment Tower Deployment in Region 3: Two Zones in May 2016 ... 62
A.16. Synthetic Control Method Results for Rapid Aerostat Initial Deployment Tower Deployment in Region 4: One Zone in September 2016 ... 62
A.17. Synthetic Control Method Results for Rapid Aerostat Initial Deployment Tower Deployment in Region 5: One Zone in December 2017 ... 63
A.18. Synthetic Control Method Results for Remote Video Surveillance System Deployment in Region 1: Three Zones in December 2014 ... 63
A.19. Synthetic Control Method Results for Remote Video Surveillance System Deployment in Region 2: 14 Zones in January 2016 ... 63
A.20. Synthetic Control Method Results for Remote Video Surveillance System Deployment in Region 3: 11 Zones in August 2016 ... 64
A.21. Synthetic Control Method Results for Remote Video Surveillance System Deployment in Region 4: Six Zones in January 2018 ... 64
A.22. Synthetic Control Method Results for Remote Video Surveillance System Deployment in Region 5: Four Zones in August 2018 ... 64

Summary

Securing and managing U.S. borders and enforcing U.S. immigration laws are two core U.S. Department of Homeland Security (DHS) missions. Addressing the unlawful flow of people across U.S. borders is an important part of both missions. At the border, U.S. Customs and Border Protection (CBP) employs what we call collectively *border-enforcement measures*—the set of resources, actions, and policies used to carry out its missions. Border-enforcement measures include tactical infrastructure, technology, personnel, and policies, such as the consequences that can be imposed as a result of unlawful entry.

DHS has been continuously called on to evaluate the effectiveness or impact of the measures it employs to secure the border, such as surveillance technology or tactical infrastructure. Doing so entails tackling two challenges. First, it requires identifying or estimating appropriate *metrics* that can be used to measure outcomes that capture important aspects of border security or outputs of border-enforcement actions and policies. Second, it requires establishing a *causal connection* between border-enforcement actions or policies and such metrics. Efforts to identify and estimate relevant metrics, which would convey important information about the state of border security, have been steadily advancing. By comparison, less work appears to have been done on the second challenge.

This study applied quasi-experimental statistical methods to the second challenge, while the metrics problem was outside its scope. In particular, we investigated the impact of deploying each of several surveillance technology assets (integrated fixed towers [IFTs], remote video surveillance systems [RVSSs], and tactical aerostat systems [TASs][1] and rapid aerostat initial deployment [RAID] towers) on the levels of Border Patrol apprehensions of unlawful border-crossers across the zones of the southwest border. Surveillance technology is thought to advance the DHS mission at the border chiefly through two channels: boosting the U.S. Border Patrol's situational awareness (i.e., enabling the detection of more border-crossers) and deterring migrants from crossing the border through the surveilled areas. Through this analysis, we have

1 In this report, when we refer to *TAS*, we refer to the aerostat only.

demonstrated whether and how certain statistical modeling methods can be used to assess both kinds of effects of border-enforcement measures.

Methodology

Researchers working with observational data have developed a variety of methods to identify the effects of any given factor on outcomes that are driven by a multitude of factors. Specifically, researchers look for quasi-experimental settings, which allow well-controlled comparisons that can be plausibly interpreted in causal terms. We employed some quasi-experimental methods here—notably, *difference-in-differences* regression models and *synthetic control methods* (SCMs). These methods aim to answer the counterfactual question that is crucial to assessing effectiveness or impact: What would have happened to a given metric (here, U.S. Border Patrol apprehensions) had some "treatment" (here, surveillance technology assets) not been deployed? Each statistical method has limitations, and our approach was to tailor analysis to address the limitations, and employ more than one modeling approach with different limitations and different advantages. Because solving the metrics problem was outside the scope of our research, we employ the best available proxy metric: Border Patrol apprehensions, which can reflect changes in the unlawful migrant flow or the rate at which the Border Patrol apprehends unlawful migrants. Although the meaning of apprehension trends is somewhat ambiguous, we observe that any positive effects on apprehension levels identified through statistical analysis would be difficult to explain without reference to improved situational awareness, and any negative effects would be difficult to explain without reference to deterrence.

Key Findings

Although the picture presented by the two quasi-experimental statistical modeling methods we employed (difference-in-differences analysis and SCMs) is not perfectly clear, the analyses do suggest several conclusions. First, the analyses suggest strongly that **the deployment of IFTs depressed apprehension levels of all migrants**. This result is consistent across models and methods. Although we caution against a focus on exact magnitudes of the effects, our analyses suggest that the effect was not trivial. We emphasize the ambiguity of apprehensions as a metric and the inevitable uncertainty inherent in applying statistical methods to a relatively small number of deployments. Nonetheless, we conclude that there is strong evidence for the presence of a deterrent effect as migrants choose to avoid areas surveilled by IFTs—a proposition for which there is also qualitative evidence outside the data. Still, we recognize the possibility that some of the effect might be due to changes in other aspects of border enforcement in response to surveillance technology, such as a shifting of Border Patrol personnel to areas without such technology. It has been suggested that recent migrants from Central America, a majority of whom seek asylum, are less concerned than migrants from Mexico are about avoiding apprehensions by the Border Patrol and should therefore be less deterrable by such measures as surveillance technology. However, we do find significant and consistent negative effects on apprehensions of Central American migrants, whereas the estimated effects on apprehensions of Mexicans are not as marked. This effect could reflect smugglers' incentives or variability in the Central American migrant population; it might also reflect responses to the changing treatment of asylum-seekers postapprehension since 2016.

Findings are less clear for the remaining technologies. Results do suggest that the effects of some—and potentially all—of the other surveillance assets are in the other direction, toward elevating apprehension levels. Of these findings, evidence is most consistent with regard to TASs. It is also possible that RAID towers and RVSSs produced upward pressures on apprehension levels. These findings point to the likelihood that, for TASs and perhaps the other surveillance assets, the boost to the Border Patrol's situational awareness dominates any deterrent effects.

Table S.1 summarizes our findings and our qualitative assessment of the strength of the evidence for each finding. We adopted the following scale for the strength of the evidence behind each of the potential effects of surveillance technologies:

- Evidence for a particular finding is **strong** if the estimated effect is consistent—in direction and statistical significance—across methods and different model specifications.
- Evidence for a particular finding is **moderate** if there are no marked inconsistencies in the estimated effects across methods and model specifications but results are inconclusive for some models.
- Evidence for a particular finding is **weak** if there are inconsistencies and inconclusive results. (For these cases, we rely on the result of the soundest analysis available.)

Although we cannot offer a decisive answer as to what distinguishes IFTs from other technologies considered here, the differences in their effects as detected in our analysis are likely to be a combination of (1) material differences among the technology assets and the places where they are deployed and (2) a function of the limitations of data and methodology. With regard to 1, the surveillance technology types have different capabilities and are concentrated geographically within specific sectors, with dissimilar border-crossing landscapes and conditions. Thus, the extent to which the assets are visible and recognizable to migrants and to which those assets improve on preexisting detection capabilities likely varies across technologies and locations. With regard to 2, the requirements of statistical methods and the characteristics of the data

Table S.1
Summary of Findings Across Models, with Qualitative Assessments of the Strength of Evidence

Technology	Estimated Effect on Apprehension Levels	Apprehended Population	Comparative Strength of Evidence
IFT	Negative	Total	Strong
	Negative	Central American	Strong to moderate
	Negative or none	Mexican	Strong to moderate
TAS	Positive	All	Moderate
RAID tower	Positive	All	Weak to moderate
RVSS	Positive	Total	Weak

NOTE: The estimated effect specified is on the "total" apprehended population, a subset of that population (Central American or Mexican), or "all" three categories (total and the two subsets); it is possible that the estimated effect on the total population is negative or positive without a corresponding statistically discernible effect on either subset of that population.

might have made reaching consistent results more difficult for some technologies: For example, the relatively small number of some surveillance assets (notably, of TAS and RAID towers) could make it difficult to separate the effects of technology from noise.

Implications

We found evidence that the impact of surveillance technology is likely uneven across different technology types. The strongest evidence suggests that the likely deterrent effect on migrant crossings through areas surveilled by IFTs overwhelms any boost to situational awareness. The finding of a deterrent effect is important in light of recent trends, which create the perception that the many changes to border enforcement since 2016 have not markedly affected unlawful migration (as measured by apprehensions). Our findings suggest that, although border-enforcement measures differ in their impacts, at least some probably affect migrant behaviors. This kind of causal analysis could be important for identifying measures that affect border security in specific, intended ways.

More broadly, in this study, we have demonstrated that quasi-experimental statistical methods hold promise for helping DHS understand the effects of border-enforcement measures, although they also have limitations. Using apprehensions as a metric can be problematic and ambiguous; nonetheless, in this study, we have demonstrated that, even when used with such a metric, these statistical methods can shed some light on the complex problem of effectiveness. This is so especially if statistical analysis is supplemented with qualitative evidence outside the data, such as observations from the field.

Most importantly, this kind of analysis carries the potential to help operational commanders and policymakers understand and anticipate the effects of border-enforcement measures. This can inform **decisions about investments into technology and infrastructure** by quantifying some of the benefits of such investments. It can inform **operational decisions** about the deployment of various resources and assets, facilitating more-effective deployment patterns. And such analysis can usefully inform **operational planning and policy responses** to migrants' adaptations to the deployment of various resources and assets. Overall, it helps DHS generally, and CBP in particular, advance the aims of making decisions based on "quality data and analysis" and "measuring and ensuring success" in their missions.[2]

---

[2] CBP, *Strategy 2020–2025*, Publication 0883-0419, April 2019a, pp. 19, 23.

Acknowledgments

We gratefully acknowledge those individuals within the U.S. Department of Homeland Security who generously provided their time and insights to this project. In particular, we are grateful to Jay Visconti, Rodney Washburn, Ntina L. Cooper, Keith A. McManus, Ryan Riccucci, Marc Rosenblum, and Ronald Bellavia for helping us focus the project and obtain data. We would also like to thank U.S. Customs and Border Protection's Analytics, Modeling, and Simulation Division for serving as sponsor and for its support throughout this project—particularly, Kamela White and Isaac Maya, who moved on from Analytics, Modeling, and Simulation while this project was in progress. In addition, we owe a debt to our Homeland Security Operational Analysis Center internal reviewers, Carter C. Price and Shelly Culbertson, for their insight and feedback throughout the research process. We also benefited from the expert advice of Blas Nuñez-Neto. Finally, we would like to thank Lara Schmidt, Jeremy M. Eckhause, Heather J. Williams, and Henry H. Willis for the tremendous counsel and oversight they provided to our project.

Abbreviations

ACS	American Community Survey
CBP	U.S. Customs and Border Protection
DHS	U.S. Department of Homeland Security
DID	difference in differences
FFRDC	federally funded research and development center
FY	fiscal year
GAO	U.S. Government Accountability Office
HSOAC	Homeland Security Operational Analysis Center
IFT	integrated fixed tower
OIG	Office of Inspector General
POE	port of entry
RAID	rapid aerostat initial deployment
RGV	Rio Grande Valley
RTM	Repeated Trials Model
RVSS	remote video surveillance system
SCM	synthetic control method
TAS	tactical aerostat system

CHAPTER ONE

Introduction: Studying the Effects of Border-Enforcement Measures

The U.S. Department of Homeland Security (DHS) has been continuously called on to evaluate the effectiveness of the measures it takes to secure the border and enforce immigration laws. Doing so entails tackling two challenges. First, it requires identifying or estimating appropriate *metrics* that can be used to measure outcomes that capture aspects of border security or outputs of border-enforcement actions and policies. Second, it requires establishing a *causal connection* between border-enforcement actions or policies and such metrics. Efforts to identify and produce relevant metrics, which would convey important information about the state of border security, have been steadily advancing—producing estimates, such as the total unlawful migrant flow across the U.S.–Mexico border and the rate at which U.S. Customs and Border Protection (CBP) apprehends illicit border-crossers. By comparison, less work has been done on the second challenge, that of establishing a causal connection between what DHS and CBP do at the border and such metrics.

Establishing causal connections in real-world settings with data that imperfectly capture complex and multifaceted phenomena, such as unlawful cross-border migration, is difficult. Yet, social scientists and statisticians have developed a variety of statistical methods that can help establish causal connections in such settings. In this study, we applied two types of the so-called quasi-experimental methods to one set of border-enforcement measures: surveillance technology. This analysis helped us investigate whether, and to what extent, such statistical modeling methods can be used to identify the effects of surveillance technology and of other border-enforcement measures more broadly. The study thus serves as a demonstration of concept, which could help operational commanders and policymakers understand and anticipate the effectiveness of border-enforcement measures, such as surveillance technology.

This chapter describes the background, scope, and setting for the present study and lays out the two-part challenge of evaluating the impact or effectiveness of border enforcement. Chapters Two and Three explain in nontechnical terms the statistical methods employed, describe the data used in the study, and present and interpret the results of the series of models estimated. The final chapter in the report seeks to spell out both the limitations and the promise of the statistical methods employed to help advance CBP's aims of making decisions based on "quality data and analysis" and "measuring and ensuring success" in its missions.[1]

Policy Background

Securing and managing U.S. borders and enforcing U.S. immigration laws are two core DHS missions. Addressing the unlawful flow of people across U.S. borders is an important part of both missions. At the border, CBP employs what we call collectively *border-enforcement measures*—the set of resources, actions, and policies used to carry out its mission. Border-enforcement measures include tactical infrastructure, surveillance and other technology, and personnel. They also include the different consequences that can be imposed as a result of unlawful entry, such as voluntary return or criminal prosecution for federal immigration crimes.

Border-enforcement measures are expected to achieve certain effects that improve border security and reduce or redress violations of immigration laws. Notably, many measures are intended to better detect, interdict, or deter unlawful cross-border migration flows. In addition to these intended effects, border-enforcement measures can also produce adaptations, such as the displacement of migrant flows from one route to another. An understanding of these effects is important to inform DHS's investments decisions and planning processes as to which resources to deploy where and when. Ultimately, DHS's capacity to respond effectively to the unlawful flows of people across the border requires an accurate picture of what impact border-enforcement measures have on the federal government's ability to detect, interdict, and deter such flows.

Documents issued as part of audits and oversight have continuously emphasized the need for CBP to develop metrics of performance or indicators of impact to provide an objective way to track the effectiveness of border-enforcement measures or their contribution to border security. For example, in 2011, the U.S. Government Accountability Office (GAO) recommended that CBP "determine the mission benefits to be derived from implementation of the Arizona Technology Plan," which entailed deployment of surveillance assets.[2] In 2014, GAO reported that CBP fulfilled the first recommendation but "had not developed key attributes for performance metrics for all surveillance technologies to be deployed."[3] In 2017, the DHS Office of Inspector General (OIG) noted the recognition, at least since its 1993 Sandia National Laboratories study, that, "to ensure [that DHS] is continually improving its capabilities and securing the border in an evolving threat environment, it needs to consistently and accu-

---

1 CBP, *Strategy 2020–2025*, Publication 0883-0419, April 2019a, pp. 19, 23.

2 GAO, *Border Security: Progress and Challenges with the Use of Technology, Tactical Infrastructure, and Personnel to Secure the Southwest Border*, Washington, D.C., GAO-18-397T, March 15, 2018, pp. 6–7.

3 GAO, 2018, pp. 6–7.

rately measure effectiveness."[4] As of 2017, the OIG concluded that "CBP does not measure the effectiveness of its programs and operations well; therefore, it continues to invest in programs and act without the benefit of the feedback needed to help ensure it uses resources wisely and improves border security."[5] In 2018, GAO likewise concluded that "the Border Patrol has not yet used available data to determine the contribution of surveillance technologies to border security efforts" and that "CBP has not developed metrics that systematically use data it collects to assess the contributions of border fencing to its mission . . . ."[6] And in 2019, GAO reported that CBP was moving toward acting on GAO's recommendation to "develop metrics to assess the contributions of pedestrian and vehicle fencing to border security" and to "analyze available data to determine the contribution of surveillance technologies to CBP's border security efforts."[7] As the latter GAO report suggests, CBP has broadly concurred with the need to measure and assess impact, calling for "measures of performance" and "indicators of impact" for all objectives in its 2012–2016 Border Patrol strategic plan.[8] In its 2020–2025 strategy, CBP remains committed to assessing systematically whether its activities are having the expected impact.[9] Moreover, Congress has issued a mandate for DHS to develop and regularly report metrics "to measure the effectiveness of security between ports of entry," including a call to estimate the impact of some border-enforcement measures.[10]

Study Scope: Surveillance Technology Between Ports of Entry

In this study, we focused on a subset of land-based surveillance technology deployed along the southwest border. Surveillance technology is intended to advance DHS's missions primarily by helping CBP increase situational awareness—that is, "knowledge and understanding of current unlawful cross-border activity" between ports of entry (POEs)—which, in turn, enables the apprehension of those crossing illicitly.[11] Moreover, surveillance technology can potentially deter crossing over the surveilled areas by increasing the perceived probabilities of detection and apprehension. CBP

4 OIG, *CBP's Border Security Efforts: An Analysis of Southwest Border Security Between the Ports of Entry*, Washington, D.C., OIG-17-39, February 27, 2017, p. 13.

5 OIG, 2017, p. 2.

6 GAO, 2018, p. 1.

7 GAO, *Border Security: Assessment of the Department of Homeland Security's Border Security Improvement Plan*, Washington, D.C., GAO-19-538R, July 16, 2019b, p. 18.

8 OIG, 2017.

9 CBP, 2019a, p. 23.

10 Public Law 114-328, National Defense Authorization Act for Fiscal Year 2017, December 23, 2016, § 1092.

11 DHS, 2019, p. 18; CBP, 2019a.

presently employs various mobile and stationary surveillance technology assets for these purposes. Stationary technology includes integrated fixed towers (IFTs), remote video surveillance systems (RVSSs), unattended ground sensors (seismic and image), and tactical aerostat systems (TASs). Mobile technology includes mobile surveillance capability, mobile video surveillance systems, agent-portable surveillance systems, and thermal imaging devices.

Although tests conducted to ensure that technology meets operational requirements and field experiences suggest that surveillance technologies have their intended effects, systematic and rigorous study of whether and to what extent deployed surveillance assets advance CBP's mission remains an underexplored question, to our knowledge.[12] In 2011 and 2014, GAO recommended that CBP develop analytic efforts to address this question; as of 2018, GAO reported limited progress toward this goal.[13] This study represents an effort to conduct preliminary investigations of the effects of several stationary surveillance technologies on aspects of border security relevant to CBP's mission. We focus in particular on the effects of IFTs, RVSSs, and TASs and RAID towers.

IFTs consist of surveillance equipment, such as ground surveillance radars and surveillance cameras, mounted on 80- to 160-foot-tall stationary towers, which assists in providing long-range, persistent surveillance to detect, track, identify, and classify items.[14] IFTs provide data, video, and geospatial locations of items of interest.[15] These surveillance assets were deployed in the Tucson sector, between 2015 and 2018, with further deployments planned for 2020.

RVSSs consist of "multiple daylight and infrared cameras and a laser illuminator mounted on 3- to 90-foot-tall monopoles, 120-foot-tall fixed towers and buildings"; a relocatable RVSS is mounted on an "80-foot-tall tower, which is on a steel platform trailer and can be relocated to other sites."[16] Unlike the IFTs, "the RVSS does not

---

[12] For example, CBP certified that the IFT program met operational requirements "based on a review of test results and agent feedback from the IFT deployment in Nogales, Arizona," which reportedly "confirm that the IFT system adds surveillance capability, increasing situational awareness and officer safety" (CBP, "Integrated Fixed Towers Certified," March 22, 2016). At least one ongoing effort, by the Johns Hopkins University Applied Physics Laboratory, is germane but is likely to be taking an approach to this problem from the methods in the present study. See DHS, *Department of Homeland Security Border Security Metrics Report*, February 26, 2019, pp. 9–10.

[13] In 2018, for example, GAO stated that, "While the Border Patrol has taken action to collect data on technology, it has not taken additional steps to determine the contribution of surveillance technologies to CBP's border security efforts" (GAO, 2018, p. 7).

[14] GAO, *Southwest Border Security: Border Patrol Is Deploying Surveillance Technologies but Needs to Improve Data Quality and Assess Effectiveness*, Washington, D.C., GAO-18-119, November 2017b, p. 3; GAO, 2018, p. 5.

[15] OIG, 2017.

[16] GAO, 2018, p. 5.

include radar."[17] Many RVSS towers are part of a legacy system and date to before the year 2000; however, some are newer, with the latest set of these having been deployed since 2014. RVSSs are most often deployed right along the border.

The Tactical Aerostats and Relocatable Towers Program consists of aerostats (tethered, lighter-than-air platforms), towers, cameras, and radars to provide surveillance over a wide area. The program's six tactical aerostats come in one of three models (persistent threat detection system; the persistent ground surveillance system; and the smallest, the rapid aerostat initial deployment [RAID] system), and 17 relocatable RAID towers are arrayed along the southwest border.[18] In this report, we use *TASs* to refer to the aerostats and *RAID towers* to refer to the latter towers. Smaller aerostats "operate at altitudes from 500 to 5,000 feet and monitor ground activity with radars, infrared and electro-optical cameras."[19] Most of the aerostats and towers are or have been deployed in the Rio Grande Valley (RGV), with one aerostat and fewer towers in the Laredo sector.[20]

The selection of technology assets for the present analysis was driven largely by data availability and quality. Notably, because these assets are all fixed, their deployed positions are relatively well known. However, it is also worth noting that these technologies include two of the three highest-cost technology programs and represent some of the most recently fielded assets.[21]

The Challenge of Evaluating the Effectiveness or Impact of Border-Enforcement Measures

Identifying the contribution of particular border-enforcement measures to the DHS mission, or their effectiveness, is difficult for two main reasons: the much-discussed metrics problem and the (somewhat less discussed) causality problem. The maturation of various methods for causal inference in the quantitative social sciences, at least in theory, makes these methods obvious candidates for attacking the second problem.

---

[17] GAO, 2017b, p. 3.

[18] GAO, *Border Security: DHS Surveillance Technology, Unmanned Aerial Systems and Other Assets*, Washington, D.C., GAO-16-671T, May 24, 2016.

[19] Dave Long, "CBP's Eyes in the Sky: CBP's Tethered Aerostats Keep Watch for Trouble from 10,000 Feet," CBP, undated.

[20] GAO, 2016, p. 17.

[21] GAO, 2017b, p. 3.

The Metrics Problem

First, there is the much-noted problem of metrics, or quantifiable indicators that capture relevant aspects of border security. As DHS explains in its latest border metrics report, metrics can be categorized into four types:

- *inputs*, which are the "resources acquired or expended to secure the border," such as the number of U.S. Border Patrol agents deployed, miles of fencing, or numbers of surveillance resources—i.e., these capture a portion of what we are calling *border-enforcement measures*[22]
- *activities*, which are "actions taken to secure the border," such as apprehensions of unlawful migrants or "pounds of narcotics seized"[23]
- *outputs*, which are "immediate results of enforcement activities as they relate to the border security goals," such as "the rate at which intending unlawful border crossers are apprehended or interdicted, and the accuracy of screening results for travelers and goods at POEs"[24]
- *outcomes*, which are "the ultimate impacts of border security policies," including, most importantly, "the numbers of illegal migrants and quantities of illegal goods entering the United States" and "the ease with which lawful travelers and goods pass through POEs."[25]

As the border metrics report explains, the metrics that are consistently and readily available based on observation pertain to inputs into border security and border-enforcement activities. These could be useful for "workload management and tactical decision-making," but these metrics themselves "typically provide limited insight into the state of border security."[26] Thus, even if determining the impact of some border-enforcement measures on inputs or activities were readily feasible, this would likely not capture the impact on meaningful aspects of border security.[27] By contrast, outputs and outcomes would likely provide more insight and are better suited to serve as metrics of performance or impact.[28] However, outcomes and outputs are not directly observable, given the clandestine nature of the cross-border activities.[29]

---

[22] DHS, 2019, p. 5.

[23] DHS, 2019, p. 5.

[24] DHS, 2019, p. 5.

[25] DHS, 2019, p. 5.

[26] DHS, 2019, p. 5.

[27] Of course, in this report, we suggest that investigating the impact of surveillance technology on apprehensions, an activity metric, is not meaningless, even if not fully informative.

[28] DHS, 2019, p. 5.

[29] DHS, 2019, p. 5; see also OIG, 2017, p. 8.

Outcomes and outputs are also difficult to estimate by means other than observation. Nonetheless, options exist, and efforts have been made to do so.[30] All such efforts produce metrics that are limited in some ways and, notably, are not well-suited for statistical analysis that aims to establish causal connections. For example, DHS has calculated the "effective interdiction rate," which relates Border Patrol interdictions (apprehensions) to the known flow. The latter is based on Border Patrol agents' observations of migrants who turned back to return to the country from where they entered (turn backs) and those who crossed the border and got away (got aways). The key conceptual limitation of this metric is that it does not account for the unknown flow. Moreover, according to CBP officials, data on turn backs and got aways is not sufficiently consistent for use in cross-sector comparisons.[31]

Another example is DHS's current attempts to estimate the unlawful flow and the apprehension rate, which builds on a study conducted for DHS by the Institute for Defense Analyses, itself based on the Repeated Trials Model (RTM) demonstrated by prior researchers (including Joseph Chang, a co-author of the present study).[32] However, these efforts, as DHS reports, remain "a work in progress, as DHS is not yet able to validate certain modeling assumptions or to quantify the uncertainty around its new estimation techniques."[33] These efforts tend to produce estimates at levels of granularity that are insufficient for the kinds of statistical approaches we used to identify the relationship between border enforcement and the outcomes or outputs, and this tendency is crucial. For example, building on the RTM, DHS's border metrics report offers estimates of the total unlawful flow and the apprehension rate—but only annually and by sector.

---

30 For overviews, see Office of Immigration Statistics, DHS, *Efforts by DHS to Estimate Southwest Border Security Between Ports of Entry*, September 2017, and Andrew R. Morral, Henry H. Willis, and Peter Brownell, *Measuring Illegal Border Crossing Between Ports of Entry: An Assessment of Four Promising Methods*, Santa Monica, Calif.: RAND Corporation, OP-328-OSD, 2011.

31 GAO, *Southwest Border Security: Additional Actions Needed to Better Assess Fencing's Contributions to Operations and Provide Guidance for Identifying Capability Gaps*, Washington, D.C., GAO-17-331, February 2017a, pp. 44–45. Nonetheless, as we suggest in the next section, these data can be analyzed to some extent in follow-up analyses.

32 DHS, 2019, p. 64. For the Institute for Defense Analyses study, see John W. Bailey, Sarah K. Burns, David F. Eisler, Clare C. Fletcher, Thomas P. Frazier, Brandon R. Gould, Kristen M. Guerrera, Terry C. Heuring, Brian Q. Rieksts, Bryan Roberts, and John E. Whitley, "Assessing Southern Border Security," Institute for Defense Analyses, Paper NS P-5304, May 2016. For prior research on the RTM, see Thomas J. Espenshade, "Using INS Border Apprehension Data to Measure the Flow of Undocumented Migrants Crossing the U.S.–Mexico Frontier," *International Migration Review*, Vol. 29, No. 2, Summer 1995, pp. 545–565, and J. Chang, S. Calkins, D. McGarvey, N. Kallfa, L. Nguyen, M. Roberts-Lahti, and P. Keller, Homeland Security Studies and Analysis Institute, *Strategic Sampling Framework for Surveillance Mission Needs Analysis*, prepared for U.S. Customs and Border Protection, U.S. Department of Homeland Security, Homeland Security Studies and Analysis Institute Report RP 14-14-03, 2016, Not available to the general public.

33 DHS, 2019, p. 6.

Another available metric of output has particular relevance to surveillance technology. CBP has been keeping track of "assisted apprehensions"—that is, apprehensions that were made pursuant to detection or tracking by a given asset (from surveillance to canines)—to "track the contribution . . . to its mission activities" of technology assets, such as tactical aerostats.[34] As of June 2014, the Border Patrol informed its agents that the "asset assist" data field in the Enforcement Integrated Database has become mandatory.[35] GAO suggests that, "[w]hen used in combination with other relevant performance metrics or indicators, these data could be used to better determine the impact of CBP's surveillance technologies on CBP's border security efforts and inform resource allocation decisions."[36] However, there are at least two obstacles for using this metric to assess the impact of technology assets. First, in part because of the recency of systematic efforts to record these data, it is thought to have inconsistencies. Second, although they "track the contribution of [surveillance technology] to its mission activities" over time, these metrics do not enable us to study impact of deploying the technology asset in the first instance. By definition, asset assists are not, and cannot be, available before the asset is deployed, which prevents comparing some aspect of border security before and after that deployment.

DHS is also working on other approaches that could offer other measures of outputs, such as CPB's Tracking, Sign Cutting, and Modeling system, which "connects between agents' actions (such as identification of a subject through the use of a camera) and results (such as an apprehension) and allow for more comprehensive analysis of the contributions of surveillance technologies to the Border Patrol's mission."[37] Tracking, Sign Cutting, and Modeling might enable, for example, the construction of a metric that tracks the enforcement rate relative to identified subjects of interest.

Fundamentally, there is no consensus on, or systematic availability of, a specific output or outcome metric that can be used to evaluate the performance of border-enforcement measures, including surveillance technology. Even the available input and activity metrics have limitations, which is unsurprising given the magnitude and complexity of the phenomena they seek to capture and the multitude of agents responsible for producing them.[38] This has led some experts and stakeholders to conclude that, given this challenge, "basic questions about changes in immigration flows and the effectiveness of policies and programs cannot be authoritatively answered," which means that Congress and DHS continue to "have difficulty evaluating existing policies

[34] GAO, 2016.

[35] GAO, 2018, p. 7.

[36] GAO, 2018, p. 7.

[37] GAO, 2018, p. 8.

[38] For an overview of limitations of available metrics, see GAO, *Border Security: DHS Should Improve the Quality of Unlawful Border Entry Information and Other Metric Reporting*, Washington, D.C., GAO-19-305, March 21, 2019a.

and programs or make informed choices about the costs and benefits of current and potential investments."[39]

The Causality Problem

Even in the presence of relevant metrics, identifying how a specific border-enforcement measure affects that metric is difficult. At times, some government literature implies that evaluating the effectiveness of border-enforcement measures can be simply a matter of finding and tracking the right performance metrics.[40] However, trends in any given metric do not ordinarily speak for themselves: Although metrics can contribute to an assessment of the state of border security generally, they cannot in themselves constitute an assessment of the effects or effectiveness of particular border-enforcement measures.

Apprehension trends—the most widely reported activity metric pertaining to the border—illustrate this point. Historically, the buildup of an impressive border-enforcement machinery—including the full suite of border-enforcement measures noted here—was accompanied by a decline in apprehensions from a peak of 1.6 million in 2000 to a historic low of 304,000 in 2017.[41] That decline was broadly seen as an indication of declining total unlawful migration flows, attributed at least in part to successful deterrence created by beefing up U.S. border enforcement.[42] Since 2017, however, apprehensions surged, more than tripling in 2019 thus far—again seen as an indication in surges of migrants—against the background of unprecedented attention and resources being poured into U.S. border enforcement.[43] In other words, devoting more resources to border enforcement has correlated with both decreases and increases in apprehension levels. Thus, without more analysis, these apprehension trends cannot reveal much that is unambiguous about the effectiveness of border enforcement generally.

Even accurate outcome measures, such as the volume of unlawful migration (rather than activity measures, such as apprehensions), cannot in themselves answer the causal questions because the volume of migration "only partially depend[s] on border security policies."[44] As a large body of research demonstrates, migration decisions are

---

[39] Marc R. Rosenblum and Faye Hipsman, *Border Metrics: How to Effectively Measure Border Security and Immigration Control*, Migration Policy Institute, January 2016.

[40] See, for example, DHS, 2019, p. 5.

[41] U.S. Border Patrol, "United States Border Patrol: Nationwide Illegal Alien Apprehensions Fiscal Years 1925–2018," c. March 2019.

[42] See, for example, Randy Capps, Doris Meissner, Ariel G. Ruiz Soto, Jessica Bolter, and Sarah Pierce, *From Control to Crisis: Changing Trends and Policies Reshaping U.S.–Mexico Border Enforcement*, Washington, D.C.: Migration Policy Institute, August 2019.

[43] Capps et al., 2019, p. 5.

[44] DHS, 2019, pp. 5–6.

affected by "numerous factors outside enforcement agencies' control": push factors in the origin countries, such as security threats or economic pressures; pull factors, such as economic opportunities in the United States; the costs of migration that stem from factors other than border enforcement; and demographics of the sending countries. The proverbial absence of "natural experiments" and the impossibility of conducting randomized controlled trials make it challenging to separate the effect of a specific border-enforcement measure from the effects of all the other factors that affect migration trends and patterns.

Measures of the direct outputs of enforcement actions are also not in themselves sufficient to assess the effectiveness of those enforcement actions. For example, consider the observational apprehension rate, a measure of the share of detected migrants that the Border Patrol is able to apprehend, which is defined as the ratio of apprehensions to the known unlawful entries (or the sum of apprehensions and got aways). As the border metrics report explains, declines in that rate do not mean that the Border Patrol has become less effective at interdictions but rather reflect "increased domain awareness—i.e., that through technological advances, the agency has improved its awareness of illegal entry attempts (known got aways)—rather than experienced a drop in enforcement effectiveness."[45] This ambiguity characterizes virtually any metric that has been advanced to capture some aspect of border security and border enforcement.

A solution to the metrics problem was outside the scope of this study. That is, we did not attempt to generate new indicators that could be used to assess the impact of surveillance technology on the border-enforcement mission. Nor do we use some of the more innovative of the existing approaches to measuring outputs or outcomes—such as the aforementioned estimates of the total flow or the apprehension rate.[46]

Instead, in this study, we employed existing, imperfect metrics to demonstrate potential ways of using statistical methods developed for causal inferences to address the second problem. With our analysis, we have highlighted both the potential and the limitations of applying so-called quasi-experimental methods to questions of border-enforcement effectiveness. We then sought to identify what might mitigate those limitations and make these methods more useful in assessing the effects of border-enforcement measures on metrics of interest. Because of the noted metrics problem, any relationships we found between the deployment of surveillance assets and the imperfect metric we employed (Border Patrol apprehensions) would not have a wholly unambiguous interpretation. We address the ambiguities in more detail in the next section but note here that qualitative evidence outside the data themselves can help make sense of the results of statistical analysis.

---

[45] DHS, 2019, p. 9.

[46] This is so for two previously noted reasons: First, those estimates are not available at the level of granularity needed for the present purposes; and second, as DHS's border metrics report states with regard to the unlawful migrant flow estimates, "DHS is not yet able to validate certain modeling assumptions" (DHS, 2019, p. 6).

The DHS OIG has also made an argument that CBP should use apprehensions as a metric of effectiveness for border-enforcement measures, in the absence of other alternatives.[47] One thing we can do through this study is demonstrate the potential and limitations of employing apprehensions as proxy measure. With the potential for expanded data collection and estimation of additional metrics by DHS or CBP, the same methods can be applied to less ambiguous impact indicators. Ultimately, a meaningful assessment of performance or impact of border-enforcement measures would have to grapple with both the metrics and the causality problems. But efforts to tackle each problem separately can lay the groundwork for solving both problems in a meaningful and operationally useful manner.

The Expected Effects of Surveillance Technology

The key and immediate effect expected from the deployment of surveillance technology is increased situational awareness, or the "knowledge and understanding of current unlawful cross-border activity."[48] That is, surveillance assets should allow Border Patrol agents to better detect people crossing the border illegally.[49] Better detection, in turn, is believed to improve officer safety and boost the probability for apprehending a greater share of crossers in that it "enabl[es] Border Patrol agents to more efficiently and effectively respond to border incursions," according to a senior U.S. Border Patrol official.[50] Translating these expected effects into hypothetical metrics, we should expect that deploying a new surveillance asset—all else being equal—would place upward pressures on the detection and apprehension rates (i.e., detections and apprehensions relative to the migrant flow).

However, increased situational awareness—and, more importantly, the *perception* that surveillance would increase the probability of apprehension—could also affect migrant behavior (as well as the behavior of smugglers and others who cross the border for reasons other than migration). As migrants learn that a particular area is covered by surveillance and perceive (rightly or wrongly) that the odds of apprehension on particular routes have increased, those who wish to avoid detection will alter their behavior and seek to avoid the surveilled areas. That is, deploying surveillance assets could also produce deterrence (or terrain denial).[51] Deterrence might mean that migrants

---

[47] OIG, 2017.

[48] GAO, 2018, p. 7; DHS, 2019, p. 18.

[49] DHS, 2019, p. 9.

[50] CBP, 2016. In this study, we did not examine the presumption that surveillance improves officer safety.

[51] For arguments that surveillance should produce deterrence, see, for example, Bryan Roberts, *Measuring the Metrics: Grading the Government on Immigration Enforcement*, Washington, D.C.: Bipartisan Policy Center, February 19, 2015.

abstain from crossing the border in the first instance, but, more likely, it would lead border-crossers to adapt their routes or tactics to avoid surveillance—such as crossing around the area that is surveilled. Translating this effect into hypothetical metrics, we should expect that deploying a new surveillance asset would place downward pressures on the total flow of unlawful migration through the surveilled area—again, all else being equal.

Testing Expected Effects with Available Metrics

Testing these two expected effects is a challenge. First, the metrics problem means that we do not have available measures of either the detection and apprehension rates or the total flow. These unobserved metrics, however, are closely tied to the level and changes in an available metric: apprehensions made by the Border Patrol. Although historically, apprehensions were viewed as a proxy for total illegal migration flows (a valid assumption if the apprehension rate does not change), they can also be seen as a proxy for the apprehension rate (a valid assumption if the total flow does not change). Thus, it is useful to spell out the expected effects of both increased situational awareness and deterrence on observed apprehension levels under certain explicit assumptions, which we do in Table 1.1.

Observed trends in apprehensions might be a result of changes in the apprehension rate or the changes in the total flow—for example, decreases in apprehensions might be a result of a decrease in the apprehension rate or a decrease in total flow, while increases might be a result of an increase in rate or in total flow. If both situational awareness and deterrence are boosted by some intervention, the expected effect on apprehensions is ambiguous: A simultaneously increasing apprehension rate and decreasing flow, for example, could manifest as increasing, decreasing, or steady apprehension levels, depending on the magnitude of each change.

However, identifying the effects that deploying surveillance assets has on apprehension levels can still be a useful endeavor. If we could isolate the effects that surveillance asset deployment has on apprehensions—that is, separating those effects from the impact of all other factors that drive apprehension levels—significant effects in

Table 1.1
Expected Effects of Surveillance Technology on Unobserved and Observed Metrics

Expected Effect of	On This Unobserved Metric	On This Observed Metric	Assuming
Improved situational awareness	Increased detection and apprehension rates (apprehensions ÷ total flow)	Increased apprehension levels	All else, including total migrant flow, remains constant.
Deterrence	Decreased total flow	Decreased apprehension levels	All else, including the apprehension rate, remains constant.

either direction could give us important clues as to which of two effects is likely to be dominant. That is, if the deployment of surveillance assets caused an increase in apprehension levels, that fact could constitute good evidence that situational awareness was boosted. Such a finding would not mean that deterrence was absent completely, but it would suggest that the boost to the detection (and, thus, to apprehension) capabilities was the more significant consequence. By contrast, if the deployment of surveillance assets caused a decrease in apprehension levels, that fact would offer good evidence of deterrence. As above, this does not mean that situational awareness was not enhanced at all but that deterrence was considerable enough to outweigh manifestations of an increase in detection and apprehension rates. Of course, any other changes in border-enforcement measures that are made simultaneously with the deployment of surveillance technology would complicate matters. For example, a surveillance asset might be treated as a substitute for personnel, so some border patrol agents might be reassigned away from the area covered by surveillance. This possibility would complicate inferences about the effects of deploying surveillance assets, and the likelihood of such occurrences should be considered and investigated.

The Expectation of Nonuniform Effects

Effects of surveillance technology might not be uniform across different technologies or different migrant subpopulations. Most straightforwardly, the technical detection capabilities are not the same across different technologies: For example, as specified above, RVSS surveillance does not have radar, whereas IFTs and TASs do. Different assets might also not be equally visible to would-be border-crossers: For example, IFTs are, on average, taller than RVSS towers, which means that they might have greater visibility to migrants and produce a more marked deterrent effect. Moreover, different capabilities of the various surveillance technologies meant that each was deemed suitable for different environments, which also affects both the reach of surveillance and the visibility of the asset.[52] Thus, although it is difficult to generate grounded a priori expectations about how exactly expected effects would differ across technologies, both the expected boost to situational awareness and deterrence might not manifest to the same extent. For these reasons, in modeling, it is preferable to treat each technology type as a distinct intervention or "treatment," the effects of which are of interest.

Similarly, it might not be sound to expect all migrants to be uniformly deterred by the increased odds of being apprehended that new surveillance assets portend. Notably, the changing composition of the migrant population roughly in the past five to ten years might have resulted in less responsiveness of a growing share of migrants to the deterrent effects of surveillance. Prior to this period, migration across the southwest border was dominated by young males of Mexican origin seeking to work in the United States. And according to some (qualitative) expert assessments, the modern-

[52] GAO, 2017b, pp. 8–9.

ization and strengthening of border-enforcement measures worked to reduce illegal crossings of this migrant population.[53] Beginning in about 2012, however, families and unaccompanied minors from the Northern Triangle (i.e., El Salvador, Guatemala, and Honduras) came to constitute a growing share of the migrant population as the numbers of young Mexican males continued to decline. This migrant population has been primarily seeking asylum, which means that some have actively sought out the Border Patrol to turn themselves in.[54] These migrants, therefore, might not have any reason to avoid the higher odds of detection. Such an expectation is boosted by some CBP experiences: For example, Border Patrol agents in the Tucson sector have reported that several large groups of Central American family units and minors use the same crossing point in a surveilled part of the Tucson sector in succession and surrender to the Border Patrol without evasive attempts.[55] By contrast, migrants from Mexico likely continue to have an interest in evading detection and might thus be expected to be deterred from taking the route through a newly surveilled area of the border. This suggests a theoretical expectation that surveillance would produce a more marked deterrent (i.e., negative) effect on apprehension levels of Mexican migrants than on those of Central American migrants. For these reasons, in modeling, it is preferable to examine the effects on these two major subcategories of migrants separately, as well as on total apprehension levels.

---

[53] See, for example, Capps et al., 2019, p. 8.

[54] For an overview of the push factors underlying Central American migration, see Capps et al., 2019.

[55] See, for example, CBP, "231 Central Americans Surrender to Tucson Sector Border Patrol," media release, April 30, 2019b.

CHAPTER TWO

Methodology: Identifying the Effects of Surveillance Technology, Using Statistical Methods for Causal Inference

As we noted in Chapter One, even if meaningful metrics of border security were available, the relationship between the deployment of surveillance assets and these metrics usually cannot be discerned by merely tracking the metrics. Statisticians and social scientists working with observational data have developed a variety of methods to isolate the effects of any given factor on outcomes that are driven by a multitude of factors.[1] In the absence of the randomized controlled experiments—the gold standard in understanding causality—social-science researchers look for quasi-experimental settings, which allow well-controlled comparisons that can produce plausible interpretations in causal terms. We employed some of these methods here—notably, difference-in-differences (DID) regression models and synthetic control (also called synthetic comparison) methods (SCMs). In this chapter, we offer a nontechnical explanation of each method (with a more technical explanation contained in the appendix).

In general, these methods are designed to answer the counterfactual question that is crucial to assessing effectiveness or impact outside an experimental setting: What would have happened to a given factor (here, apprehensions) had some asset not been deployed? No statistical method can answer this question with complete confidence across contexts; indeed, each method has considerable limitations. Our approach was therefore to identify the limitations that are most salient in this context, tailor analysis to address the limitations, and employ more than one modeling approach with different limitations and different advantages. Even if no single method can invariably offer a clear and robust answer, conclusions are on firmer ground when supported by different modeling approaches. And identifying the limitations and the potential of causal analysis in absence of natural experiments is vital for a path forward.

---

[1] In the discussion of statistical methods, the term *outcome* is employed generically to denote a (quantifiable) result or consequence, rather than in its specialized meaning offered in Chapter One's discussion of the metrics problem.

Difference-in-Differences Design

One way to assess causal effects is to leverage the fact that surveillance assets are deployed in some, but not all, border areas (zones, stations, or sectors) at a given time.[2] Using the DID method, one can compare changes in an outcome over time between area where a surveillance asset was deployed (the treated area) and an area where it was not (the control area). The comparison of data from treated and control areas, before and after deployment, helps distinguish the effect of asset deployment (i.e., the treatment) (1) from the effects of other changes that occur at the same time and (2) from the durable differences between areas with and without assets.

Consider a simple example: Suppose that, in month 1, there were 50 apprehensions in zone A and 30 apprehensions in zone B. A surveillance asset was then deployed in B but not in A, and, in month 2, there were 60 apprehensions in zone A and 45 apprehensions in zone B. The difference from month 1 to month 2 in treated zone B was 15 more apprehensions, while the difference in the untreated, control zone A was ten more apprehensions. The results from using a DID method would suggest that the surveillance asset was responsible for five additional apprehensions (15, the change in B, minus 10, the change in A). That is, the estimated effect of deploying surveillance is obtained from the *difference in the change* in apprehension levels. Importantly, (relatively) time-invariant factors that affect apprehension levels—such as the generally higher levels of migrant flows through zone A than through zone B, the presence of a geographic obstacle to crossing in zone B, or any number of fixed or slow-changing characteristics that make the two zones different—are controlled for (or taken into account). The same in the case for factors that affect apprehension levels in both A and B—such as an economic downturn in the United States, which lowers the pull of crossing the border generally, whether it is in zone A or zone B. Unless something else that might affect apprehension levels changed from month 1 to month 2 in only one of the two zones, it is plausible to conclude that the five additional apprehensions resulted from the surveillance asset.

This method can be generalized to the case of multiple time periods, areas, and deployed assets and estimated by means of a regression. This is the case with the data at hand, in that each type of surveillance technology was deployed at various dates in various zones, and we have data on apprehensions for a considerable period before and for at least some time after each asset was deployed.

Although attractive, the DID method has its limitations. The first limitation is a central assumption that must be made about trends in the outcome examined—here, in apprehensions. The "parallel-trends" assumption is that, in the absence of treatment,

---

[2] The area of responsibility of the U.S. Border Patrol follows the hierarchy of sector, station, and zone. The southwest border consists of nine sectors, more than 90 stations, and about 700 zones.

the treated and control groups would have followed the same trend over time.[3] In the example above, the assumption means that, in absence of treatment, zone B would have increased from 30 to 40 apprehensions, paralleling the increase from 50 to 60 in untreated zone A.

Such an assumption is almost certainly problematic in the present context. Migration trends are not identical along the length of the southwest border, with various surges and dips affecting some and not other parts of the border. In addition, border-enforcement resources are arguably deployed where they are deemed to be needed, which might mean worsening trends in border security before their deployment. If surveillance assets are deployed to areas with apprehensions that are rising more steeply than in areas to which resources are not deployed, for example, declines in that rate after deployment could be a reversion toward the mean, rather than wholly the effect of surveillance. Efforts to model the effects of border-enforcement measures need to grapple with these problems; otherwise, the estimated effects will be biased. Thus, we explore options for relaxing the parallel-trends assumption for the DID models presented here.

The second limitation goes beyond the theoretical assumptions behind DID models: The uncertainty of estimates of treatment effects is likely to be understated (i.e., statistical significance will likely be overstated).[4] Therefore, we interpret the degree of confidence returned by our DID models with caution.

Synthetic Control Methods

Another way to construct a counterfactual is by resorting to an SCM. SCMs involve the development of a so-called synthetic control, which is an artificially constructed comparison unit produced with a weighted combination of untreated zones. The intuition is to construct a synthetic comparison zone that is as similar to a treated zone as possible, in terms of specified factors—which makes for a more controlled and convincing comparison.[5] Specifically, if control units are constructed to match the trends

---

[3] DID methods make other assumptions as well; here, we focus on the central one that likely presents a problem. For further discussion, see Joshua David Angrist and Jörn-Steffen Pischke, *Mostly Harmless Econometrics: An Empiricist's Companion*, Princeton, N.J.: Princeton University Press, 2008, pp. 227–243.

[4] For more detail, see the appendix.

[5] See Noémi Kreif, Richard Grieve, Dominik Hangartner, Alex James Turner, Silviya Nikolova, and Matt Sutton, "Examination of the Synthetic Control Method for Evaluating Health Policies with Multiple Treated Units," *Health Economics*, Vol. 25, No. 12, December 2016, pp. 1514–1528; Alberto Abadie, Alexis Diamond, and Jens Hainmueller, "Comparative Politics and the Synthetic Control Method," *American Journal of Political Science*, Vol. 59, No. 2, April 2015, pp. 495–510.; and Michael W. Robbins, Jessica Saunders, and Beau Kilmer, "A Framework for Synthetic Control Methods with High-Dimensional, Micro-Level Data: Evaluating a Neighborhood-Specific Crime Intervention," *Journal of the American Statistical Association*, Vol. 112, No. 517, 2017, pp. 109–126.

in outcomes in the treated units prior to treatment—such as apprehension trends—concerns about the violations of the parallel-trends assumption that are present in DID methods are somewhat alleviated. If the synthetic control zone is similar enough—and has followed a similar enough trend in its apprehensions—to the zone treated with a surveillance asset, the conclusion that the divergence in the trends after deployment is a consequence of that asset becomes plausible.

Like DID, SCMs have several limitations. Unlike DID, SCMs cannot accommodate a gradual deployment of treatments, which is the case with the surveillance assets we examined. That means that our SCM analysis focused on each date or each designated "round" of asset deployments separately. Although synthetic controls were developed for settings involving a single treated unit, here we consider an extension of the original framework that allows more-granular data, wherein multiple cases can be treated.[6] SCMs also tend to not perform well in settings with a small number of treated units or a large number of matching criteria, and this limitation makes constructing a suitable matching control more difficult. Because the results obtained from SCMs are only as good as the synthetic control, poor matches produce biased and imprecise estimates of effects. We note also that both DID and SCM models presented practical limitations in the present study setting: Given a relatively large number of zones and months present in our data, implementing the methods is computationally intensive.[7]

Synthesizing Multiple Methods

Because each of these (and indeed, all) quasi-experimental statistical methods have limitations, our approach was to consider results from multiple modeling approaches. To help mitigate these limitations and paint a more robust picture of the patterns that underpin our data, we ran an array of sensitivity analyses—that is, alternative model types and specifications. We concluded that results that were present throughout all analyses, rather than under singular specifications, were more convincing. In particu-

[6] Alberto Abadie, Alexis Diamond, and Jens Hainmueller, "Synthetic Control Methods for Comparative Case Studies: Estimating the Effect of California's Tobacco Control Program," *Journal of the American Statistical Association*, Vol. 105, No. 490, June 2010, pp. 493–505; Robbins, Saunders, and Kilmer, 2017.

[7] In particular, more-robust procedures for evaluating uncertainty in our data, such as bootstrapping and permutation methods for DID models, are largely infeasible in our study because of computational complexities (although these methods should be strongly considered should statistical modeling become a routine approach to evaluating effects of border-enforcement measures).

lar, we adopted the following scale for the strength of the evidence behind each of the potential effects of surveillance technologies:

- Evidence for a particular finding is **strong** if the estimated effect is consistent—in direction and statistical significance—across methods and different model specifications (or sensitivity analyses).
- Evidence for a particular finding is **moderate** if there are no marked inconsistencies in the estimated effects across methods and model specifications but results are inconclusive for some models (e.g., using the SCM, we could not find a closely matching synthetic control).
- Evidence for a particular finding is **weak** if there are inconsistencies and inconclusive results. (In these cases, we report the result of the most robust specification available.)

CHAPTER THREE

What Do Data and Statistical Analysis Tell Us?

In this chapter, we describe the data employed for the analysis and explain in non-technical terms what our analysis suggests, as well as what it cannot reveal. (A more technical treatment is offered in the appendix.) The results of this analysis indicate consistently that deploying IFTs depresses apprehension levels relative to what would have been expected in the absence of the asset. We emphasize the ambiguity of apprehensions as a metric and the uncertainty inherent in applying statistical methods to a relatively small number of deployments; nonetheless, we conclude that the findings constitute strong evidence for the presence of a deterrent effect. Results are more inconclusive for the other surveillance assets under consideration, but there are suggestions that TASs (and, to a lesser extent, RAID towers and RVSSs), unlike IFTs, elevate apprehension levels where deployed, relative to those in other zones. The latter finding points to the likelihood that, for some surveillance assets, the boost to situational awareness dominates any deterrent effects. Although a systematic investigation of the reasons for the apparently different effects of different technology types was outside the scope of this study, we point to potential explanations, which could be explored with further research.

Describing the Data

The Data and Data Transformations

In this study, we relied on two main sets of data that CBP provided, which we transformed to create a single data set. The first data set is pulled from the e3 portal, which CBP operates to collect data related to its law-enforcement activities and which is integrated with U.S. Immigration and Customs Enforcement's Enforcement Integrated Database and DHS's Automated Biometric Identification System. This data set, to which we refer as apprehension data, contains biographic and encounter data on people interdicted and arrested by CBP at the border.[1] For each person apprehended by CBP,

[1] In addition, e3 contains biometric data for identification and verification of such people, but the data provided to us were stripped of any such identifying information.

the data set reports basic demographic characteristics, country of origin, and, crucially, where the person was apprehended. The second set of data consists of information about the location and timing (year and month) of deployment of RVSSs, IFTs, and TAS technology (which includes information on RAID towers) and some information about the capabilities of these assets.[2] These data sets were supplemented by basic socioeconomic and demographic data from the American Community Survey (ACS).[3]

The two sets of data had to be joined to be analyzed together. Thus, we created a single database in which each observation corresponded to the number of apprehensions made each month in each *zone*. The Border Patrol divides responsibility over the nearly 2,000-mile-long southwest border among nine sectors, which contain more than 90 stations or about 700 zones along the southwest border. Zones vary considerably in size and geography; some zones touch the border, whereas others are wholly on the interior of the United States (see Figure 3.1).

We chose to do our analyses at the zone level because that is the unit that best approximates the reach of a single surveillance asset. This makes a large number of areas available for comparison, which facilitates the use of statistical tools. Our joint data set at the level of individual zones pulls together information about monthly apprehension levels in each zone and information about when and in which zones surveillance assets were deployed.

The challenges in creating such a data set were twofold. First, we needed to map or assign each apprehension to a specific zone, when the zone information is not explicitly reported in CBP's data. Our main approach to this challenge was to limit our analysis to the period (post-2008) in which geographic coordinates were reported for apprehensions, which allows precise mapping to a zone. Second, we needed to determine whether each zone was covered by a surveillance asset in each month. Although the location of each asset is available, determining which zones were covered by the asset's viewshed or detection radius was less straightforward because these depend on technology, as well as the topography and conditions on the ground. Our primary approach to this issue was to deem a zone covered (or treated) by an asset if at least 30 percent of its territory fell within the asset's detection radius.[4] We also considered a nonbinary version of treatment status wherein we measured the percentage of the zone's area that was within the asset's detection radius.[5]

---

[2] We have also received data on other (predominantly mobile) surveillance technologies, but those data were not available with sufficient granularity as to timing and location to be integrated into this analysis.

[3] U.S. Census Bureau, "American Community Survey (ACS)," homepage, undated.

[4] The radius of detection itself was generally provided in the data; when it was not, we employed an approximation.

[5] Although we do not report results of models that employed this measurement of treatment, none of the conclusions we report would be altered with this variant.

Figure 3.1
Border Patrol Zones That Touch the U.S.–Mexico Border

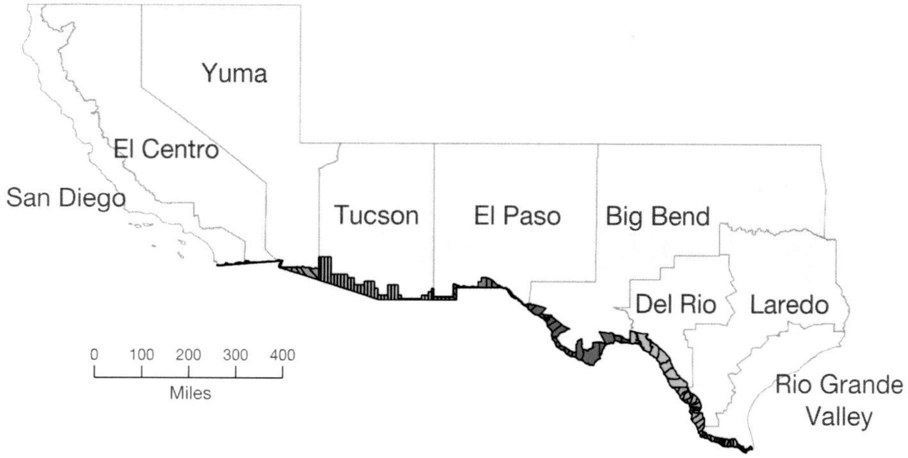

Measure	San Diego	El Centro	Yuma	Tucson	El Paso	Big Bend	Del Rio	Laredo	RGV
Border zone area, in square miles	150	157	1,404	6,515	1,839	6,477	4,671	2,978	1,588
Border, in linear miles	60	71	126	262	268	510	210	171	320
Effective zone depth, in linear miles	2.5	2.2	11.1	24.8	6.9	12.7	22.2	17.4	5.0

SOURCE: J. Chang et al., 2016.

NOTE: There are also many interior zones that do not touch the border. Effective zone depth is defined as the border zone area ÷ border miles. Rounding causes some quotients to appear imprecise.

Apprehension Trends

We begin by highlighting a few basic trends in apprehensions in recent years. Overall, apprehensions had been generally decreasing until 2017 and have risen again since, most markedly in 2019. These cumulative trends were accompanied by changing migrant composition: Whereas, in 2000, 98 percent of those apprehended at the southwest border were Mexican, in the first three quarters of fiscal year (FY) 2019, 74 percent hailed from the Northern Triangle countries of Central America.[6] Figures 3.2 through 3.4 depict trends in apprehensions by sector, between 2008 and 2019, the years surrounding the deployment of surveillance technology. These figures demonstrate that trends are not uniform across the length of southwest border; this is the case for total apprehension levels, as well as the trends in apprehensions of migrants from Cen-

[6] John Gramlich and Luis Noe-Bustamante, "What's Happening at the U.S.–Mexico Border in 5 Charts," *Fact Tank*, November 1, 2019.

Figure 3.2
Monthly Total U.S. Border Patrol Apprehensions, by Sector, 2008–2019

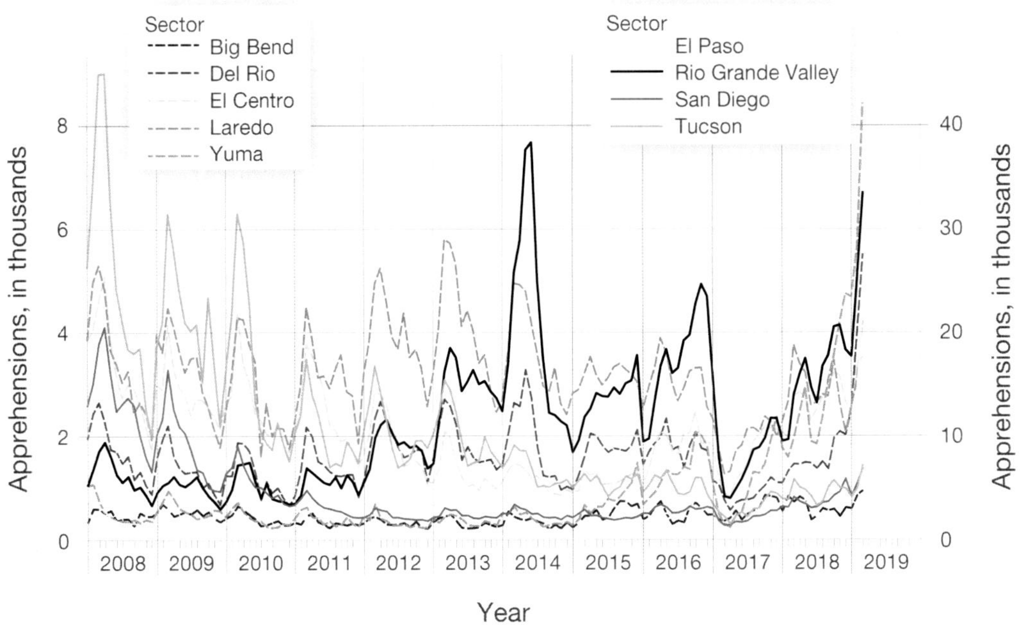

NOTE: Scale for apprehension trends for sectors depicted with dashed lines is on the left; scale for apprehension trends for sectors depicted with solid lines is on the right.

tral America and Mexico.[7] For example, apprehensions stemming from the surges in migration from El Salvador, Guatemala, and Honduras seen in 2014, 2016, and again in 2019 have been concentrated primarily in the RGV (in terms of absolute numbers); lesser surges are also visible in 2014 in Tucson, Laredo, and Del Rio and in 2016 in Tucson, and the 2019 surge was experienced across the board (Figure 3.4). Distinctive trends are also seen: For example, Tucson appears to have experienced more discrete peaks and drops than other sectors have in Central American migration. The decline in apprehensions of migrants from Mexico since 2007 has, in turn, been concentrated in the Tucson and San Diego sectors, while these have risen and then fallen somewhat in the RGV (Figure 3.3).

Deployments of Surveillance Assets

Of the surveillance technologies we studied, IFTs, TASs, and RAID towers have been deployed in the past five or so years. Figure 3.5 depicts the number of zones that have become covered (or "treated") by IFTs, TASs, RAID towers, and RVSSs since 2014.

---

7 For the purposes of this analysis, the following countries were included under Central America: Belize, Costa Rica, El Salvador, Guatemala, Honduras, Nicaragua, and Panama.

Figure 3.3
Monthly U.S. Border Patrol Apprehensions of Migrants from Mexico, by Sector, 2008–2019

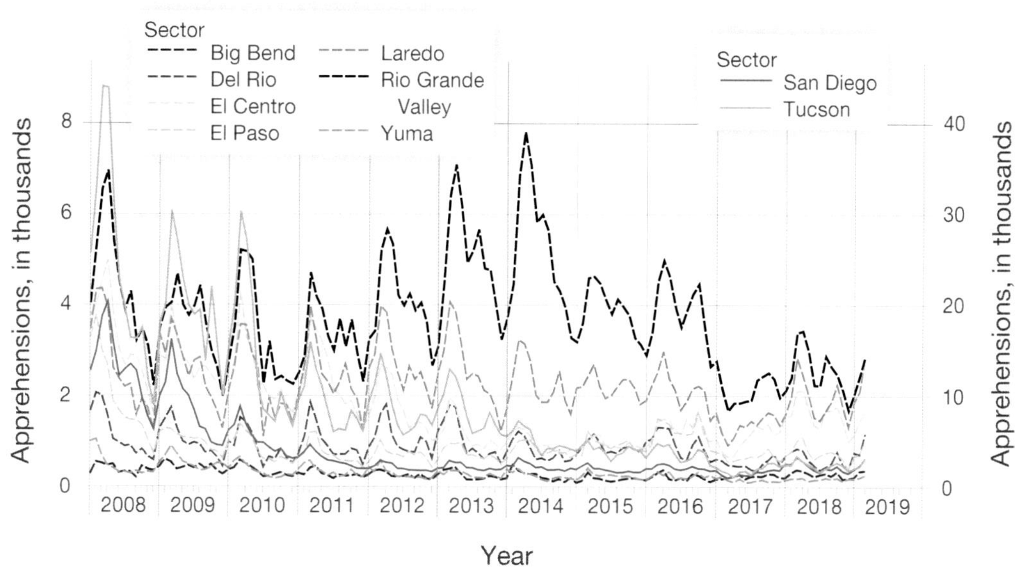

NOTE: Scale for apprehension trends for sectors depicted with dashed lines is on the left; scale for apprehension trends for sectors depicted with solid lines is on the right.

Figure 3.4
Monthly U.S. Border Patrol Apprehensions of Migrants from Central America, by Sector, 2008–2019

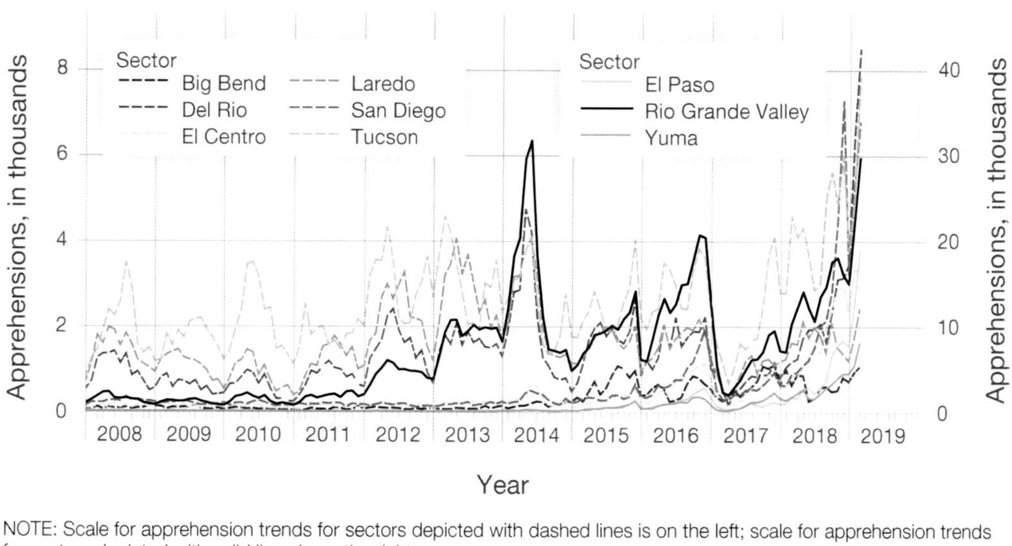

NOTE: Scale for apprehension trends for sectors depicted with dashed lines is on the left; scale for apprehension trends for sectors depicted with solid lines is on the right.

Figure 3.5
Number of Zones Treated by Integrated Fixed Tower, Tactical Aerostat System, Rapid Aerostat Initial Deployment Tower, and Remote Video Surveillance System Technologies, by Month

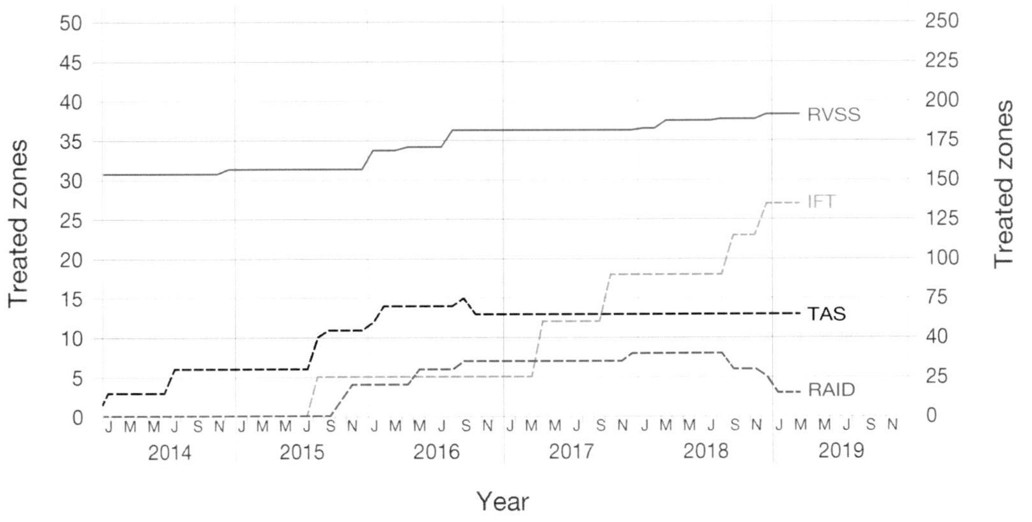

NOTE: We considered a zone "treated" by an asset if the asset's detection radius covered at least 30% of the zone. Scale for zones treated by IFTs, TASs, or RAID is on the left; scale for zones treated by RVSSs is on the right. The number of zones covered by RAID towers declines because some towers are deployed for a certain period and then removed.

Because RVSS is an older system, many such towers have been deployed since before 2000, accounting for the high starting number. However, more RVSS assets went up between 2003 and 2006 and, most recently, since 2014. Our analysis did not cover the first, legacy generation of RVSSs and focuses only on the more recent deployments.

Apprehension Trends Before and After Deployment of Surveillance Technology

Surveillance technology is not randomly or evenly distributed across the border. The later, post-2003 RVSS towers are concentrated in the San Diego, Yuma, Tucson, Laredo, and RGV sectors. IFTs cover zones primarily in the Tucson sector, and TASs primarily in the RGV sector (also touching several zones in the Laredo sector). A natural first step in understanding the relationship between surveillance and apprehensions is to examine the trends in apprehensions before and after assets are deployed. To do this, we shifted from sector-level trends down to the zone level and from a real timeline to one that is defined relative to asset deployment—that is, with each asset deploying in month 0 and the month number corresponding to the number of months before (when negative) or after (when positive) asset deployment. In this way, we might be able to observe what happened to apprehension trends before and after asset deployment—in each zone where an IFT, an RVSS, a TAS, or a RAID tower had been deployed at some point since 2014. Figures 3.6 through 3.8 depict these trends.

Figure 3.6
Apprehension Levels in the Months Before and After Deployment of Integrated Fixed Towers, by Zone

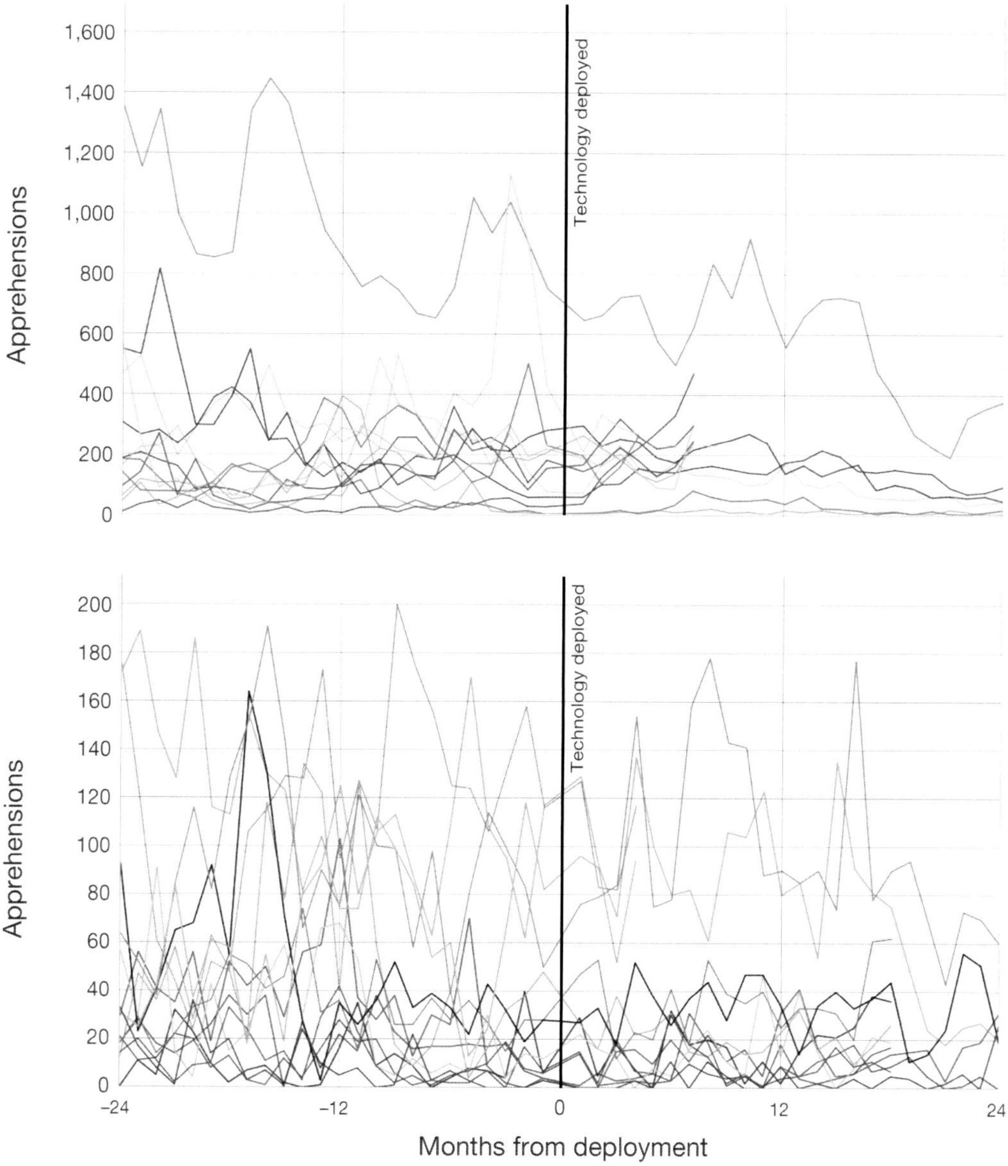

NOTE: The top panel depicts apprehension levels 24 months before and, at most, 24 months after an IFT was deployed in zones with higher absolute levels of apprehensions. The bottom panel depicts the same in zones with lower absolute levels of apprehensions. Zones are too numerous to be identified individually in a key. For some zones, less than 24 months of postdeployment data is available because of the recency of the IFT. All zones where an IFT was ever deployed are in the Tucson or El Paso sector.

Figure 3.7
Apprehension Levels in the Months Before and After Deployment of Tactical Aerostat Systems and Rapid Aerostat Initial Deployment Towers, by Zone

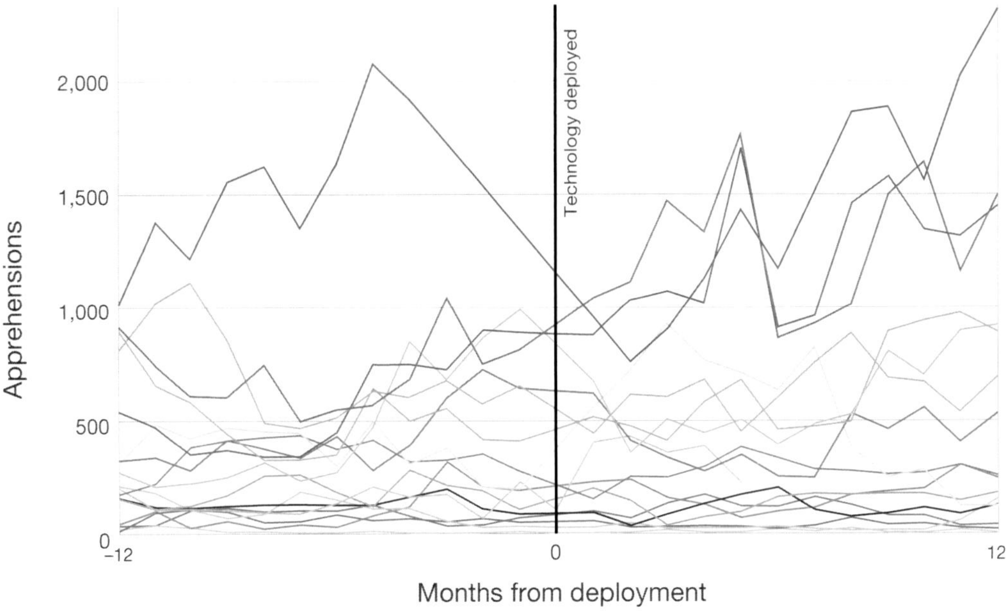

NOTE: The figure depicts apprehension levels in zones 12 months before and at most 12 months after a TAS or RAID towers were deployed. Zones are too numerous to be identified individually in a key. For some zones, less than 12 months of postdeployment data is available because of the recency of the TASs. All zones where a TAS or RAID tower was ever deployed are in the RGV or Laredo sector; there are zones where both are deployed.

Descriptive analysis is often the starting point for identifying noteworthy patterns that call for further investigation. Figure 3.6 suggests—albeit faintly—that average apprehension numbers might have declined after the deployment of IFTs, and Figure 3.7 suggests, just as faintly, the opposite effect in the wake of deployment of TASs and RAID towers. Overall, however, it is difficult to identify whether the deployment of surveillance assets is correlated with any easily discernible trends in apprehension levels. Although further descriptive analysis might yield additional insights, it would not reveal any distinctions between the impact of surveillance technology and that of other contemporaneous changes. Thus, to make that distinction, we turned to the quasi-experimental statistical methods described earlier.

Findings and Discussion

In this section, we first summarize the core findings that emerge from each set of analyses, each of which consists of multiple models. We then offer our assessment of

Figure 3.8
Apprehension Levels in the Months Before and After Deployment of Remote Video Surveillance System Towers, by Zone

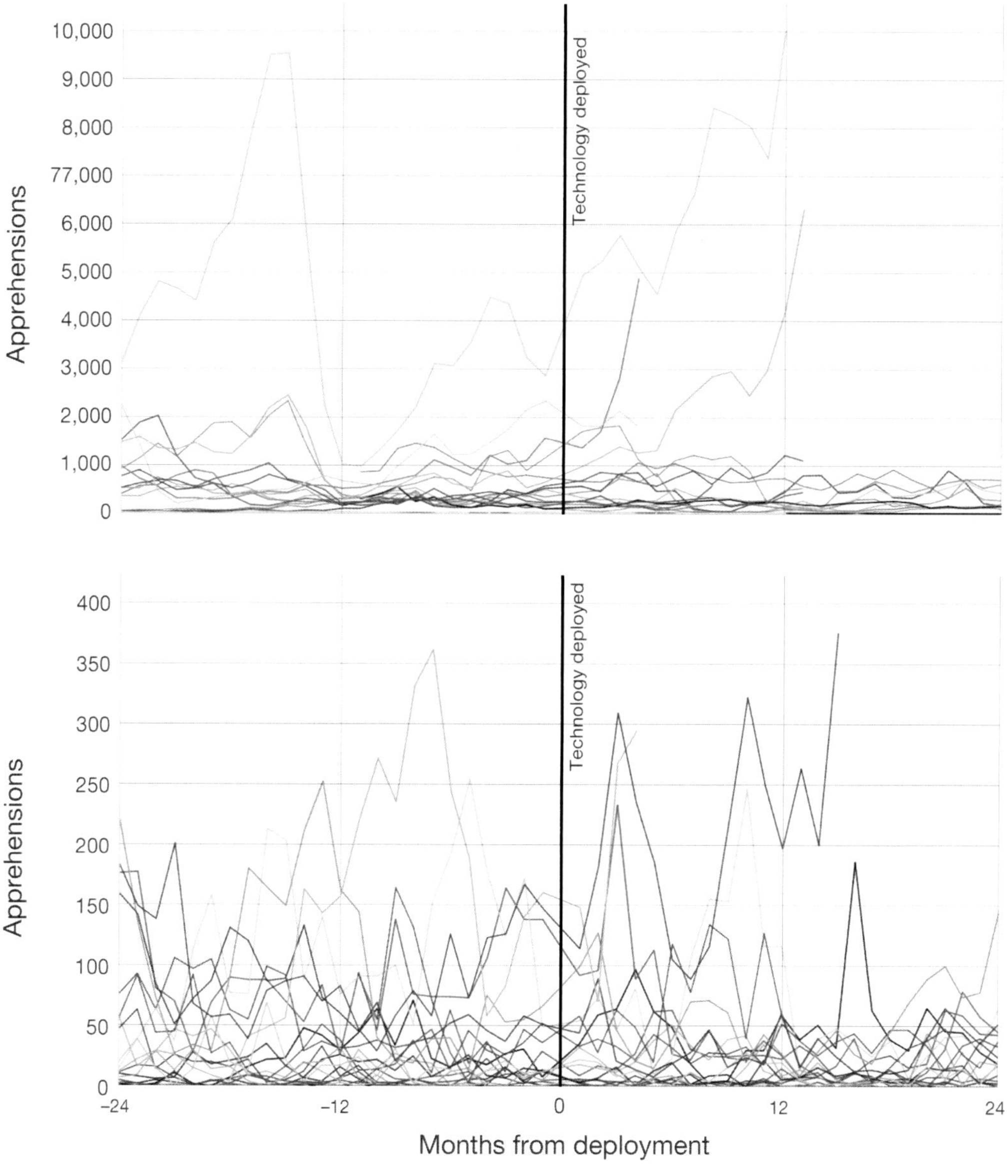

NOTE: The top panel depicts apprehension levels 24 months before and at most 24 months after RVSS was deployed—in zones with higher absolute levels of apprehensions. The bottom panel depicts the same in zones with lower absolute levels of apprehensions. Zones are too numerous to be identified individually in a key. For some zones, less than 24 months of postdeployment data is available because of the recency of the RVSSs. All zones where an RVSS was deployed post-2014 are in the San Diego, Yuma, Tucson, Laredo, and RGV sectors.

the strength of the evidence for each finding and our interpretation of what these findings mean.

Difference-in-Differences Results

We ran a series of DID regression model types at the zone level to estimate the effects that surveillance technology deployments had on apprehension levels. As suggested earlier, because the assumptions of the DID method can be demanding, we considered a variety of models to test how sensitive results are to model choices.

Table 3.1 summarizes the basic features of the model types. It contains our shorthand name for the model type, which factors are controlled or accounted for, which surveillance technologies are included, and which sectors of the border are covered in each model. Each model type contains several versions of the model (i.e., model specifications). In particular, we assessed the relationship between surveillance technology and three outcome variables: total apprehensions, apprehensions of migrants from Mexico, and apprehensions of migrants from Central America. This would allow us to test the expectation that these different migrant groups might respond differently to the deployment of surveillance technology. Each model type was also estimated with two ways of conceptualizing "treatment," or coverage of zone by a given surveillance asset: as a binary variable and as a percentage of the zone covered by the detec-

Table 3.1
Difference-in-Differences Model Summary

	Accounts for			Surveillance Technology				
Model Type	Zone Fixed Effects	Time Fixed Effects (Month to Month)	Sectoral Time Trends	IFT	TAS	RAID Tower	RVSS	Southwest Border Sectors Covered
Basic	Yes	Yes	No	All (jointly)				All (573 zones[a])
Divergent trends	Yes	Yes	Yes, but only year to year	All (jointly)				All (573 zones)
Sector-specific	Yes	Yes	Yes	Yes	TAS and RAID jointly		No	Tucson (63 zones) and RGV (58 zones)

NOTE: Each model type includes separate specifications for one of three outcomes: total apprehensions, apprehensions of migrants from Mexico, and apprehensions of migrants from Central America. The basic and divergent-trends model specifications that we discuss include all technology assets jointly (as in Model A.3 in the appendix). This ensures that the estimate of each technology's impact is not biased by the omission of other known time-varying factors. We did, however, also estimate the impact of each technology type separately (like in Model A.1 in the appendix). The models we discuss used a binary treatment variable, in which a zone was considered treated if at least 30% of its territory was covered by the detection radius of a given asset and untreated otherwise; we did, however, also estimate all models using an alternative, continuous treatment variable that captures the percentage of a zone's territory covered by the surveillance asset.

[a] This is less than the total number of zones because apprehensions do not occur in every zone.

tion radius. In all DID models presented here, we examined data beginning at least two years prior to the initial rollout of any technology considered in the model to up through one year following the final rollout of the technology.[8]

The models in what we call basic DID models include a set of variables that indicate each zone and each month under analysis, or zone and time fixed effects. Including zone fixed effects accommodates the fact that some zones generally tend to see more apprehensions than others, on average. Including time fixed effects accommodates border-wide trends in apprehensions observed across time, which means that the results do not conflate the effects of trends, such as seasonal fluctuations, and the effect of technology. In short, the model produces the effects of technology deployments by comparing the changes in apprehension levels before and after assets are deployed in treated and untreated zones.

These basic models, however, rely on the noted "parallel trends" assumption, which holds that, once we account for the different baseline levels of apprehensions in each zone, deviations from parallel trends are due only to the deployment of the surveillance technology considered here. This is likely not the case—for one thing, other border-enforcement measures have been applied to various sectors or zones in the same time period. As Figures 3.2 through 3.5 show, apprehension trends differ across sectors generally. In particular, apprehension trends in Tucson (where IFTs are deployed) and in the RGV (where TASs and RAID towers are deployed) stand out. Notably, in Tucson, apprehensions of Mexican migrants appear to have declined more precipitously than in other sectors since 2008. Tucson's trends in apprehensions of migrants from Central America also display more peaks and drops than trends in other sectors do. And in the last few months of our data, Tucson experienced a less pronounced increase in total apprehensions than some other sectors did.[9] The RGV was the locus of the surges of Central American migration since 2014; it has also experienced more-radical ups and downs in its trends than most other sectors have. These aggregate trends are doubtless a result of multiple factors and raise the possibility that the basic DID models would pick up differences between trends in Tucson or the RGV, where much of the technology is located, and elsewhere, where most of the comparison zones are located.

Thus, we amended the basic DID model to relax the parallel-trends assumption and accommodate divergent trends to some extent. What we call the divergent-trends

---

[8] An exception to this rule is that the data series for any model that incorporates an RVSS starts at December 2012. The initial rollout of RVSSs occurred prior to the start of our data (at the beginning of FY 2000); the choice of December 2012 was optimal for our analysis when taking into consideration long gaps in the rollout pattern of RVSSs. Specifically, for models involving only IFTs, the time range of the analysis is August 2013 to March 2019. For models involving only TASs, the time range of the analysis is January 2012 to December 2016. For models involving only RAID towers, the time range of the analysis is September 2012 to February 2017. For any model involving RVSSs (including models that incorporate the technologies jointly), the time range of the analysis is December 2012 to March 2019.

[9] See also Arizona Public Media, "Tucson Sector Border Patrol Chief on Trends Along Southern Border," September 13, 2019.

models allow each sector to follow different year-to-year trends (see Model A.4 in the appendix). This would allow us to distinguish effects of surveillance technology from any shocks in a given year that affect apprehension levels in some but not all sectors, such as developments in countries of origin that produce migrant surges along certain routes, other border-enforcement measures that target particular sectors, or actions by criminal cartels on the Mexican side of the border that make particular routes more dangerous for migrants.

Figure 3.9 depicts the point estimates—that is, as the estimated percentage by which apprehension levels are lower or higher than they would have been without the surveillance technology—and 95-percent confidence intervals—that is, the range of values in which the estimated effect falls with the probability of 95 percent—produced by the basic model. Figure 3.10 does the same for the divergent-trends models.

The results represented here point to the importance of assumptions and modeling choices. As Figures 3.9 and 3.10 show, the estimated effects are not identical for the basic and divergent-trends models. First, we highlight the one result in which the direction and the statistical significance of the result are the same across both model types: Zones where IFTs were deployed had *fewer* apprehensions in the period following deployment than they would have if IFTs had not been deployed in those zones at

Figure 3.9
Difference-in-Differences Regression Results, Basic Model

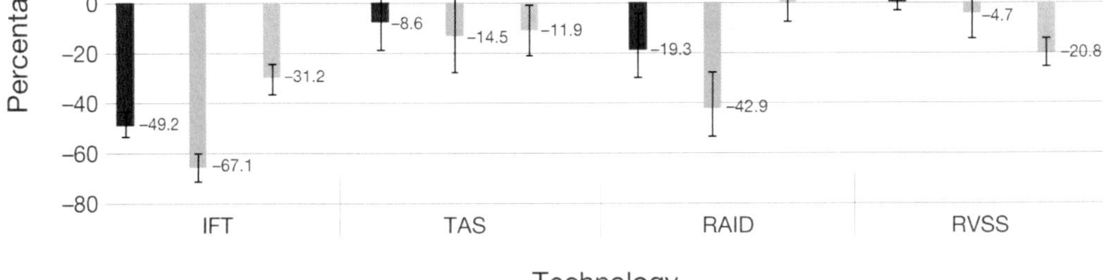

NOTE: Each bar represents the estimated effect (specified as a percentage) produced by the basic model with a binary treatment that includes all surveillance technology types together. Green bars represent estimated effects on total apprehensions; orange bars represent estimated effects on apprehensions of Central American migrants; blue bars represent estimated effects on Mexican migrants. I-bars represent 95% confidence intervals. Results are based on the analysis of 573 zones over 76 months.

Figure 3.10
Difference-in-Differences Regression Results, Divergent-Trends Model

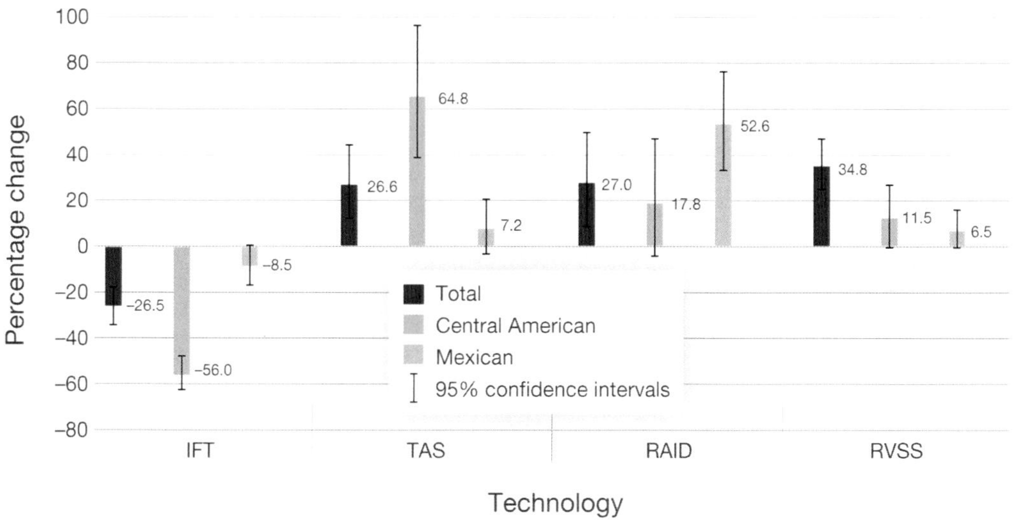

NOTE: Each bar represents the estimated effect (specified as a percentage) produced by the divergent-trends model with a binary treatment that includes all surveillance technology types together. Green bars represent estimated effects on total apprehensions; orange bars represent estimated effects on apprehensions of Central American migrants; blue bars represent estimated effects on Mexican migrants. I-bars represent 95% confidence intervals. Results are based on the analysis of 573 zones over 76 months.

those times.[10] This is the case for total apprehensions, as well as those of Mexican and Central American migrants. With the divergent-trends model, the more robust of the two types, we estimate that zones with IFTs experienced on the order of 27-percent fewer apprehensions (with the 95-confidence interval ranging from 18 percent to 34 percent) in the postdeployment period than they would have without the deployment. Both models show that the effect is squarely negative with 95-percent confidence; the exception is the effect on Mexican migrants estimated using the divergent-trends model, which is more modest in magnitude and where the actual effect could well be about 0 (Figure 3.10).

For the remaining surveillance technologies, the estimated effects are not in the same direction: Although the basic model suggests a *decrease* in apprehension levels for some apprehensions (i.e., the effect is negative), once we account for different sectoral trends in the divergent-trends model, results indicate that deployment of TASs, RAID towers, and RVSSs corresponded to an *elevation* in apprehension levels. For TASs, this effect is discerned chiefly on total apprehension levels and apprehensions of Central American migrants, with the effect on migrants from Mexico being statistically indistinguishable from 0 (as can be seen from the relatively large confidence interval,

[10] Point estimates referenced here result from multiple specifications with the binary treatment variable; they are offered to give a sense of the approximate magnitude of the effect but do not convey confidence intervals.

which includes 0). For RAID towers, the statistically detectable effect is on total apprehensions and apprehensions of migrants from Mexico only, with the effect on Central American migrants being indistinguishable from 0 (as shown with relatively large confidence intervals). RVSSs, for their part, appear to be followed by elevated total apprehensions, but no subset of these was affected at a statistically discernible level; as shown, 95-percent confidence intervals include 0 in both cases.

The reversal of the estimated direction of impact for these technologies from the basic models that assume parallel trends underscores the crucial importance of assumptions—in particular, demonstrating the importance of relaxing the parallel-trends assumption. We therefore further investigated whether the above results persist if we accommodate divergence of trends in another way. As noted, apprehension trends appear to differ across sectors—and the divergent-trends model controls only for different trends year to year. However, our analysis was of monthly data, and trends can diverge within a given year: For instance, a sudden event in a sending country can produce a surge in migration to a particular sector—and thus, in apprehensions—that lasts for a few months and is followed by a significant dip. This might not change annual apprehension levels but could create month-to-month variability that affects a model's estimates of technology's effects. This means that even the divergent-trends model could be conflating the month-to-month differences (within a year) in trends across sectors with the effect of technology.

Thus, a set of what we call sector-specific models considers only a subset of the data: These models examine the effects of only the types of surveillance technology present in Tucson (IFTs) and the RGV (TASs and RAID towers) sectors. (The same kind of analysis could not easily be done with RVSSs because these are spread across multiple sectors.) Specifically, we ran two models: One incorporated only IFTs (like in Model A.1 in the appendix), and the other included TASs and RAID towers jointly. Each model used only the sector where each asset was. These models produced their estimates of effects through a comparison of the zones covered by these assets with those that were not—within that same sector. This means that they completely removed the possibility that results were picking up differences across sectors. The results, represented in Figure 3.11, are largely consistent with those from the models shown earlier.

It is encouraging that the results of the divergent-trends (Figure 3.10) and sector-specific (Figure 3.11) models are largely consistent: Both point to a significant negative effect of IFTs on total apprehensions and apprehensions of those from Central America, with a smaller (or no) effect on apprehensions of migrants from Mexico. With both the divergent-trends and sector-specific models, we estimate that total apprehension levels were more than 20-percent lower, on average, in treated zones than they would have been without the asset—with the confidence interval remaining firmly below 0. Apprehension levels of Central Americans were estimated at more than 50-percent lower, on average, by both types of models. Apprehension levels of Mexicans were less affected by IFTs, with an estimated negative impact of less than 10 percent and with

Figure 3.11
Difference-in-Differences Regression Results, Sector-Specific Models in the Tucson and Rio Grande Valley Sectors

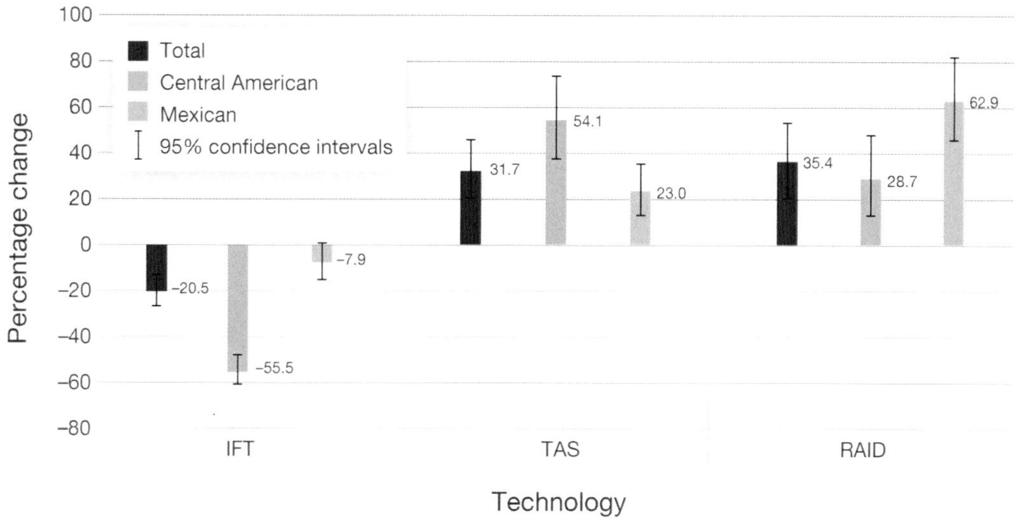

NOTE: Each bar represents the estimated effect (specified as a percentage) produced by the sector-specific model with a binary treatment that includes IFTs separately (limited to the Tucson sector) and TASs and RAID towers jointly (limited to the RGV sector). Green bars represent estimated effects on total apprehensions; orange bars represent estimated effects on apprehensions of Central American migrants; blue bars represent estimated effects on Mexican migrants. I-bars represent 95% confidence intervals. Results for IFT are based on the analysis of 63 zones over 68 months; results for TAS, of 58 zones over 68 months; and results for RAID, of 58 zones over 62 months.

the confidence interval including 0 in both types of models, which might well point to no real effects on this subcategory of apprehensions.

The deployment of TASs, by contrast, was accompanied by an elevation of more than 20 percent (for divergent trends) to more than 30 percent (for sector-specific) in total apprehensions in treated zones compared with what levels would have been without the assets (with confidence intervals of 11 to 44 percent in divergent trends and 19 to 45 percent in the sector-specific model). The deployment of RAID towers came with an elevation in total apprehensions of 27 (divergent trends) to 35 percent (sector-specific), with confidence intervals of 8 to 49 and 20 to 53 percent, respectively. The divergent-trends models (Figure 3.10) detected statistically significant effects of TASs on apprehensions of Central Americans but not of Mexicans, and of RAID towers on apprehensions of Mexicans but not of Central Americans, while the sector-specific models detected such effects for both technologies across the board (Figure 3.11).

Synthetic Control Method Results

Following our multimethod approach, we turn to SCM analysis. An SCM seeks to answer the counterfactual question of what apprehension levels would have been observed in surveilled zones in the absence of surveillance assets by comparing treated zones with synthetic control zones.[11] Synthetic control zones are constructed by matching the treated zones on outcome trends prior to treatment and basic time-invariant characteristics of zones—namely, whether the zone touches the border, its area, population, median income, and unemployment. This means that, unlike with DID, each treated zone was, by design, compared with a synthetic control zone with similar apprehension trends prior to deployment of surveillance and zone characteristics that likely affected border-crossing trends and patterns within the zone.[12]

One limitation of this method is that an SCM requires a binary treatment that is applied to all treated zones at the same time. This means that a single SCM model cannot simultaneously estimate the effects of every surveillance asset of each type that has been deployed. Thus, for IFTs, which were deployed in multiple zones on five dates, we analyze each of the five sets of deployments.[13] Other technologies were deployed on a larger set of dates, often with one asset deployed in any given month. To analyze those, we combined proximate months of deployment into broader "rounds," with the resulting loss of precision as to the exact month of deployment.[14]

As we noted earlier, another limitation of the SCM is that available data might be insufficient to find close synthetic matches. For the most part, SCM analysis of IFT deployments yielded synthetic control zones that reasonably matched the treated zones. Figure 3.12 captures the trends in total apprehensions in the zones treated at each distinct date compared with the counterfactual trend followed by the synthetic control zones. Across these graphs, the apprehensions levels in the synthetic control zones match trends in treated zones before the IFT is deployed reasonably well, which

---

[11] Robbins and Davenport, 2019.

[12] That is, each model matched on quarterly outcomes under analysis in a given model for three years pretreatment.

[13] An asset being deployed in a zone implies that at least 30 percent of the zone is within the asset's detection radius. The first deployment time of IFTs was August 2015, at which point IFTs covered five zones. The second deployment date was April 2017, at which point seven additional zones were covered; IFTs were next deployed in October 2017 in six more zones. The fourth deployment occurred in August 2018 and spanned five additional zones, and the final deployment of IFTs was in December 2018, with four more zones.

[14] Specifically, RAID towers were rolled out in five phases: The first rollout covered two zones in October 2015, the second covered two zones in November 2015, the third covered two zones in May 2016, the fourth covered one zone in September 2016, and the fifth covered one zone in December 2017. Likewise, TASs were rolled out in seven months (across a total of 16 zones), from January 2014 to September 2016. For analysis, these were condensed into two phases: the first occurring in January 2014 in six zones and the second occurring in August 2015 with deployment in ten zones. RVSSs were rolled out in 154 zones between January 2000 and January 2006. To keep the general time period studied consistent with the other analyses, we excluded these 154 zones from our SCM RVSS analyses and instead considered the next rollout, which was in December 2012, as well as six subsequent rollouts concluding in December 2018. These seven rollouts entailed 38 zones in all. For analytic purposes, we condensed these rollouts into five analytic rollouts, the first of which affected three zones and occurred in December 2014. The second analytic rollout covered 14 zones and occurred in January 2016, the third analytic rollout covered 11 zones and occurred in August 2016, the fourth analytic rollout covered six zones and occurred in January 2018, and the fifth analytic rollout covered four zones and occurred in August 2018.

Figure 3.12
Synthetic Control Method Results: Comparing Apprehension Trends in Zones Treated with Integrated Fixed Towers and Synthetic Control Zones

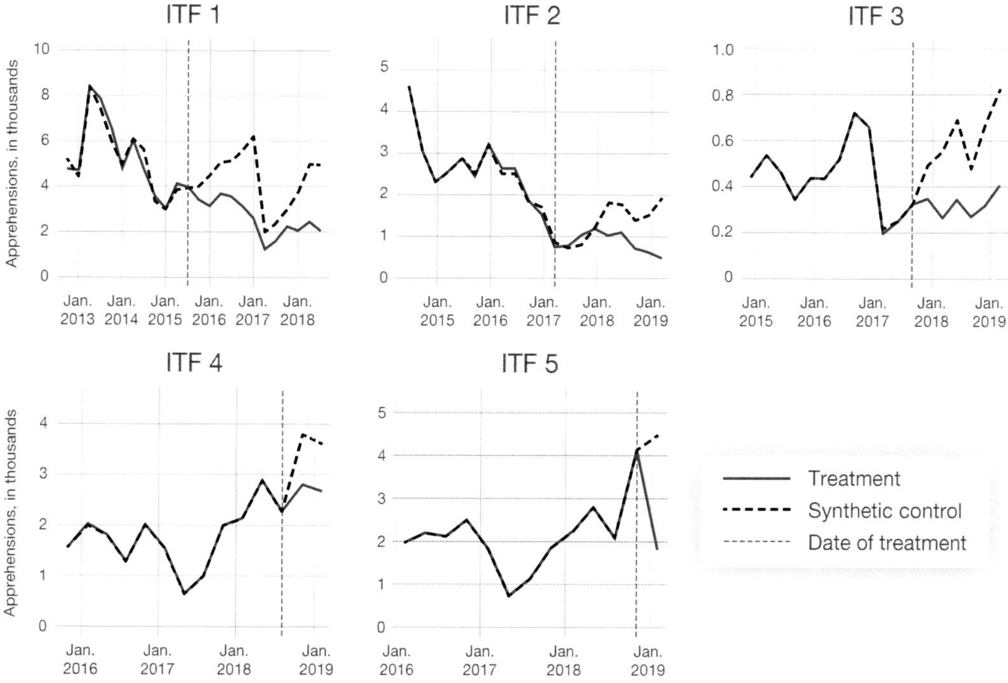

NOTE: The vertical line in each chart indicates the date of treatment (deployment of the technology). The red trend line in each chart depicts the observed trends in treatment zones, which were covered by an IFT; the black trend line depicts the estimated counterfactual trend in the synthetic control zones. The differences in apprehension levels were statistically significant for IFTs deployed on the first and last dates but not for the middle three dates. Analysis and figures were executed using microsynth software, which was developed by RAND researchers (Robbins and Davenport, 2019).

can be seen in the closeness of the two trend lines before the vertical line indicating IFT deployment. After deployment, apprehension levels in the treated zones dip below those in the comparable synthetically constructed zones, although the difference between the treated and control zones is not statistically significant in every case. Notably, zones where IFTs were deployed first (IFT 1 in Figure 3.12) experienced a statistically significant decline: Within about 24 months past deployment, apprehensions were an estimated 36-percent lower than in the synthetic control. Similarly, in zones where IFTs were deployed most recently (IFT 5 in Figure 3.8), apprehensions were estimated to be 59-percent lower within the six months of available postdeployment data, also a statistically significant difference.[15]

On the whole, SCM results support the inference from the DID analysis, that the deployment of IFTs led to decreased total apprehension levels. SCM models also con-

---

[15] We do not depict statistical significance for all the results here. See the appendix for more information.

sistently show a negative effect of IFT deployment on apprehensions of non-Mexican (Central American and other) migrants, although not always at statistically significant levels, whereas the results for Mexican migrants are less consistent. Importantly, the synthetic controls are generally less close matches to the treated zones when we examine these subcategories of apprehensions. Thus, in our cumulative assessment of findings from the totality of the analysis, we assess the evidence for the effects on the apprehensions of subcategories of migrants to be weaker than that for the total apprehension levels (findings and our assessments of confidence are offered in the next section).[16]

An SCM analysis of TASs produces more-ambiguous results, but they do, to some extent, support the results of the divergent-trends and sector-specific DID models. As Figure 3.13 illustrates, after the deployment of the first round of TASs (Aerostat 1), apprehension levels in the treated zones rose above those in the comparable synthetically constructed zones (with the estimated difference being statistically significant). The same is the case for apprehensions of Mexican and non-Mexican migrants. For all three apprehension outcomes, the differences in the trends are statistically significant and considerable in magnitude: For example, 12 months after deployment, total apprehensions were 77-percent higher, apprehensions of Mexican migrants were 68-percent higher, and apprehensions of non-Mexican migrants were 82-percent higher than the estimated levels in the absence of TAS assets (i.e., levels of the synthetic control) (see Table A.11 in the appendix). This was not the case with the second round of TAS deployments (Aerostat 2), in which trends in treated and control zones remain reason-

Figure 3.13
Synthetic Control Method Results: Comparing Apprehension Trends in Zones Treated with Tactical Aerostat Systems and Synthetic Control Zones

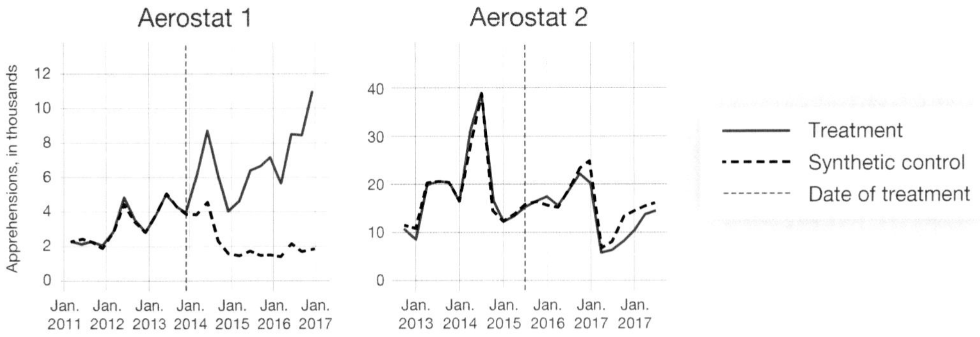

NOTE: The vertical line in each chart indicates the date of treatment (deployment of the technology). The red trend line in each chart depicts the observed trends in treatment zones, which were covered by a TAS; the black trend line depicts the estimated counterfactual trend in the synthetic control zones. The differences in apprehension levels were statistically significant for TASs deployed on the first, but not the second, round. Analysis and figures were executed using microsynth software, which was developed by RAND researchers (Robbins and Davenport, 2019).

[16] In the interest of space, we do not show the trend lines for treated and control zones for apprehensions of Central American or Mexican migrants.

ably close after deployment (see Table A.12 in the appendix for estimates). However, the estimates for the effects of the second round of TAS deployments are a result of poorer matching; thus, these do not necessarily indicate that the TAS technology had negligible effects in its latter round of deployments.

Using SCMs to identify the effects of other surveillance technologies met with less success, generally producing synthetic controls that matched treatment zones less closely, so results could be subject to bias. Figure 3.14 illustrates two of five rounds of RAID tower deployments (RAID 3 and RAID 5), in which less close matches between treated and synthetic control zones, as well as less distinct differences postdeployment, can be seen. Overall, the results were not consistent in direction and were largely statistically insignificant. Similarly, matching was poorer for RVSSs and produced inconsistent results across the five rounds of RVSS deployments: Figure 3.15 shows the results for the first round of deployments of RVSSs, revealing both a comparatively poor match in trends predeployment and ambiguous trends postdeployment.

We emphasize that this does not mean that SCM analysis decisively disconfirms what DID analysis suggests about the effects of RAID towers or RVSSs. Rather, the limitations of the methods and relevant data preclude us from drawing confident conclusions in these cases.

Interpreting the Results of Quasi-Experimental Methods

Although the picture presented by the two quasi-experimental statistical modeling methods we employed is not perfectly clear, the analyses do suggest several conclusions, supported by evidence of variable strength, as summarized in Table 3.2. First,

Figure 3.14
Synthetic Control Method Results: Comparing Apprehension Trends in Zones Treated with Rapid Aerostat Initial Deployment Towers and Synthetic Control Zones

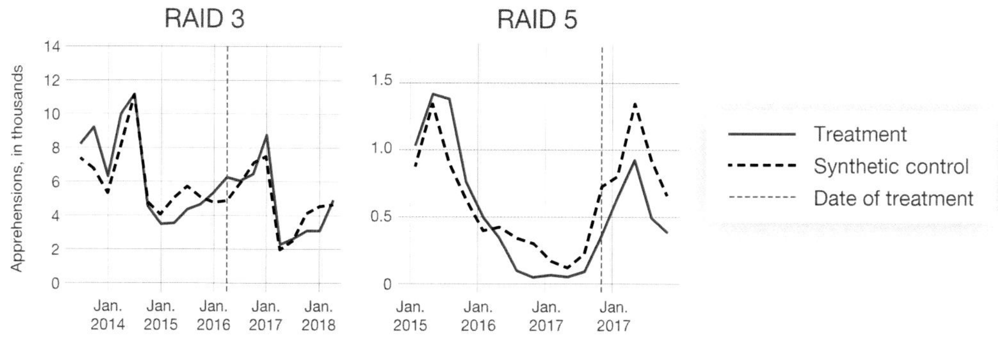

NOTE: The vertical line in each chart indicates the date of treatment (deployment of the technology). The red trend line in each chart depicts the observed trends in treatment zones, which were covered by a RAID tower; the black trend line depicts the estimated counterfactual trend in the synthetic control zones. The differences in apprehension levels were partially statistically significant (significant for 12, but not six, months postdeployment) for RAID towers deployed on the fifth, but not the third, round. Analysis and figures were executed with microsynth software, which was developed by RAND researchers (Robbins and Davenport, 2019).

Figure 3.15
Synthetic Control Method Results: Comparing Apprehension Trends in Zones Treated with Remote Video Surveillance Systems and Synthetic Control Zones

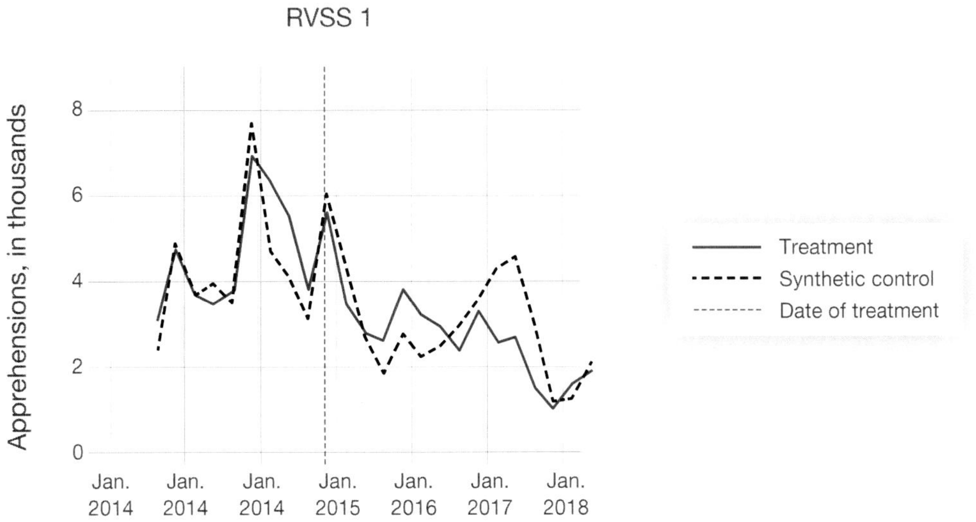

NOTE: The vertical line in each chart indicates the date of treatment (deployment of the technology). The red trend line in each chart depicts the observed trends in treatment zones, which were covered by RVSSs; the black trend line depicts the estimated counterfactual trend in the synthetic control zones. The differences in apprehension levels were not statistically significant for RVSSs deployed in this round. Analysis and figures were executed with microsynth software, which was developed by RAND researchers (Robbins and Davenport, 2019).

Table 3.2
Summary of Findings Across Models, with Qualitative Assessments of the Strength of Evidence

Technology	Estimated Effect on Apprehension Levels	Apprehended Population	Comparative Strength of Evidence
IFT	Negative	Total	Strong
	Negative	Central American	Strong to moderate
	Negative or none	Mexican	Strong to moderate
TAS	Positive	All	Moderate
RAID tower	Positive	All	Weak to moderate
RVSS	Positive	Total	Weak

NOTE: The estimated effect specified is on the "total" apprehended population, a subset of that population (Central American or Mexican), or "all" three categories (total and the two subsets); it is possible that the estimated effect on the total population is negative or positive without a corresponding statistically discernible effect on either subset of that population.

the analyses suggest strongly that the deployment of IFTs depressed apprehension levels. For total apprehension levels, this result is consistent across models and methods, which leads us to conclude that evidence for this result is strong. Although we would advise caution in interpreting the magnitude or the precise statistical significance of the effect, the range of estimates suggests that the effect was likely not trivial. All analyses also suggest a negative effect on apprehensions of Central American or non-Mexican migrants and either a negative or no effect on those of Mexican migrants. However, we conclude that the evidence for effects on these subcategories is somewhat less strong than for the total effect. Although SCM analysis produced relatively closely matching synthetic controls for models with total apprehension levels, matching was generally poorer for these subcategories. Thus, although the results on the whole are consistent with those obtained from DID methods, they could be biased because of reliance on the less close matches.

Findings are less clear for the remaining technologies. Results do suggest that the effects of some—and potentially all—of the other surveillance assets are in the other direction, toward elevating apprehension levels. Of these, evidence is most consistent for TASs, for which both methods suggest the same inference; however, SCM matching was poorer and results less consistent. Thus, we judge this inference as being backed by evidence of moderate strength. RAID towers and RVSSs might also have produced upward pressure on apprehension levels, but evidence for these effects is considerably weaker (i.e., inconsistent or inconclusive or both). We emphasize that our lack of consistent findings on the effects of the latter is not an affirmative finding of no effects.

If the effects estimated here are correct, what do they mean? As we noted, because the metrics problem was outside our scope, the metrics we studied here are ambiguous. However, it is difficult to explain the relative decrease in apprehension levels after deployment of IFT assets by reference to increased situational awareness (i.e., improved detection and apprehension rates) only. Thus, some countervailing effect must be present. Deterrence of crossings across the surveilled zones very likely accounts for at least some of the countervailing effect. Moreover, some evidence outside the data exists to support this proposition. For example, a senior CBP official based in Tucson relayed that cross-border traffic appears to change in response to new surveillance assets, as migrants begin to "walk around the viewshed" of the asset.[17] Similar accounts have been offered by journalists and others investigating border crossings: In one example, a migrant group was spotted by a recently deployed IFT in the Nogales station of the Tucson sector, and "a binoculars-wielding smuggler lookout in Mexico noticed and by cellphone directed the migrants to evade arrest by returning to Mexico," a return that Border Patrol agents observed.[18]

---

[17] Interview, Washington, D.C., October 23, 2019.

[18] Richard Marosi, "Towers and Cameras, Not a Wall, Keep Migrants from Crossing the Border into Arizona," *Los Angeles Times*, April 16, 2018.

Contrary to the expectation that Mexican migrants might be more responsive to the perception of an increased probability of detection, results tend to find a more marked effect on apprehensions of migrants from Central America. There is ample evidence of Central American migrants turning themselves in to Border Patrol agents when detected, which suggests an insensitivity to detection via surveillance. However, our analysis suggests that, at least in the Tucson sector, Central American migrants do respond to the presence of surveillance technology. The effect could reflect smugglers' incentives more than the migrants' own, or it could point to variability within the Central American migrant population. It might also reflect responses to the changing treatment of asylum-seekers postapprehension since 2016.[19]

It is important to note that statistical estimates might also be capturing aspects of the border-enforcement response to surveillance technology. New, powerful technology makes less necessary manual efforts to detect illegal cross-border activity—which, as we suggested earlier, could cause a kind of substitution effect if some Border Patrol personnel were reassigned farther away from the detection radius to areas that remain uncovered by surveillance technology. Although there are some indications that some changes to where and how Border Patrol agents operate do occur in conjunction with technology deployment, it is also unlikely that the Border Patrol would systematically reassign personnel from places with considerable detected traffic.[20] On a related note, as a CBP subject-matter expert explained, as migrants begin to adjust their paths to avoid a surveillance asset, the Border Patrol might deploy more agents to those surrounding areas—a law-enforcement adaptation to the migrant adaptation.[21] If so, the estimated magnitude of the effect includes not only the migrant response but also the enforcement response: The relative decreases in apprehension levels in the zones treated with new assets might be, in part, a reflection of the increased enforcement activity in the zones surrounding treated zones.

Why are the effects different for other surveillance technologies? Although we have less confidence in the relative elevation of apprehension levels after the deployment of TASs (and possibly the remaining technologies), we have flagged the most-likely explanations for such effects and then for the difference in the net effect of different surveillance technologies.

First, it would be difficult to explain the relative increase in apprehension levels after deployment of TAS (or other) assets without a reference to improved situational awareness—an improved ability to detect and apprehend border-crossers. This does

[19] See, for example, Randy Capps, Doris Meissner, Ariel G. Ruiz Soto, Jessica Bolter, and Sarah Pierce, *From Control to Crisis: Changing Trends and Policies Reshaping U.S.–Mexico Border Enforcement*, Washington, D.C.: Migration Policy Institute, August 2019.

[20] A senior CBP official explained that deployments of Border Patrol personnel would be responsive to detected traffic (interview, Washington, D.C., October 23, 2019).

[21] Interview, Washington, D.C., October 23, 2019.

not mean that TASs do not deter crossings at all but rather that the boost to detection and apprehensions masks any such effects. Alternative explanations for the patterns do exist. These include a change to other aspects of border enforcement simultaneous with the deployment of TASs only in the zones covered by TASs—such as an increase in the number of agents available to make apprehensions or the apportionment of mobile surveillance assets to agents at the same time. Another alternative explanation would be increases in migrant flows, concentrated on the same zones and times where TASs were deployed. We have encountered no compelling evidence for either of these possibilities. An increase in personnel also appears at odds with the general expectation that surveillance technology enables CBP to gain awareness with fewer agents on the ground. Although we think that these alternatives are not very likely, neither is impossible and, to a certain extent, can be tested with more data on border-enforcement measures.

Second, although we cannot offer a decisive answer as to what distinguishes IFTs from other technologies considered here, we point to several non–mutually exclusive candidate explanations. The differences in the statistical results are very likely to be a combination of (1) material differences among the technology assets and the places where they are deployed and (2) limitations of data and methodology. As for material differences, the surveillance technology types have different features and capabilities. For example, IFTs have a greater range of capabilities than RVSS towers, and the latter tend to be shorter than the former (80 to 160 feet for IFTs, compared with 30 to 120 feet for RVSSs). RVSS towers are also typically installed alongside infrastructure (e.g., walls and barriers). Thus, RVSS towers might be less visible to migrants, and their relatively modest capabilities might become understood by repeat players (such as smugglers), either of which would diminish the towers' deterrent potential. TASs are equipped with radio repeaters that retransmit signals from high altitude, which "instantly boost[s] communications range for agents on the ground patrolling in flat, poor-reception areas"—which could manifest as shorter times for agents to respond to detected border-crossers.[22] Moreover, different surveillance technology assets are concentrated geographically in specific sectors, with dissimilar border-crossing landscapes and conditions. Some of these conditions might facilitate deterrence in the case of IFTs (in Tucson) but perhaps mute it in the cases of TASs and RAID towers (both in the RGV) and in sectors where the later generation of RVSSs are deployed. Locations of each type of surveillance might also point to significant differences in the composition of the groups of migrants who cross the border, which might not be captured by available variables, such as national origin or demographic characteristics.

As for limitations of the data and the statistical methods, these also partly contribute to the difference in the consistency and the confidence of results across different technology types. Statistical methods work best with large amounts of data. The relatively small number of surveillance assets (notably, of TASs and RAID towers) could

---

[22] Long, undated.

hamper separating the effects of technology from noise, irrespective of the statistical approach employed. The imprecision in the data could play a role as well: RVSS data, in particular, are not as precise as data for the other technologies, with the month and year of deployment sometimes not provided. For both IFTs and RVSSs, moreover, a detection radius was not reported for each asset (as it was for TASs and RAID towers), and our approximation might be less accurate for RVSSs than it is for IFTs. Importantly, the assumptions of the quasi-experimental methods (discussed in Chapter Two) might be less tenable for some technologies than others.

CHAPTER FOUR

The Path Forward and Conclusions: Implications for the Department of Homeland Security

In this study, we investigated whether and to what extent certain quasi-experimental statistical methods developed in the social sciences can be used to answer questions crucial for evidence-based border security policies. Such statistical methods are frequently the best available means to evaluate effects of some intervention or treatment using observational data, in the absence of randomized controlled trials. Through our investigation, we have demonstrated that, although these methods cannot provide unassailable and unambiguous answers in every case, they can help to address the causality problem and produce informative evidence about the contributions of border-enforcement measures to DHS missions. Although we examined a subset of surveillance technology, the same methods can be applied to other border-enforcement measures. These methods present both promises and limitations, which we spell out in this concluding chapter, to sketch a path forward.

Limitations of Quasi-Experimental Methods and the Available Data

The limitations of the methods we employed here stem largely from the kind of data that these methods require and their assumptions. We outline these in this section.

First, statistical methods, such as DID and SCMs, are data demanding. To produce valid and informative conclusions, these methods require data to be consistent and complete. Moreover, because these methods rely on the availability of large numbers of treated and untreated units for comparisons, data must be available at a high level of granularity (such as monthly, at the zone level). This applies to data both about border-enforcement measures, such as surveillance technology, and about the relevant outcomes at the border or outputs of border-enforcement activities. As noted throughout, when this is not the case, statistical methods are unlikely to produce robust conclusions or to be employable in the first instance. We were unable, for example, to model the relationship between unattended ground sensors and apprehensions because data on that technology are available only as annual counts at the sector level. Similarly, we were unable to investigate the relationship between the deployment of surveillance assets and a more germane outcome variable—estimates of total illegal migrant flows—because estimates of the latter are not available at a sufficiently high level of granularity. And, as discussed, we limited our analysis to apprehensions largely because other theoretically relevant metrics are not available consistently and completely. For example, we did not incorporate analysis of turn backs or got aways because those data might not have been reported consistently across sectors and are therefore likely to produce misleading results.[1] This means that, to the extent that data recorded and maintained by DHS are inconsistent, insufficiently detailed, or unavailable, statistical methods will not be very useful.[2]

Second, validity of insights produced by statistical methods, such as DID and SCMs, depends on plausibility of assumptions and requirements that are stringent at times. Even where data are complete and consistent, statistical methods have their limitations. As we have emphasized throughout, every method of statistical inference will fail to produce precise and unbiased results when the data-generation process radically departs from its assumptions. For example, border-enforcement measures are often deployed in response to problematic trends—such as a surge of a particular kind of migration or other illicit cross-border activity. If areas with unique trends are systematically targeted for border-enforcement measures, be it the deployment of technology, personnel, or infrastructure, this can pose a problem for statistical modeling: DID methods, as noted, rely on the parallel-trends assumption, which is violated if all areas with worsening trends experience a given border-enforcement measure and none of the rest do. SCMs, which relax the parallel-trends assumption to some degree, still risk poor performance when this assumption is not satisfied.

A more fundamental assumption or requirement for some statistical methods, such as DID and SCMs, to produce robust results is the availability of (multiple) comparisons. This means that DID and SCMs tend to not work very well with interventions that are relatively rare because having only small numbers of treated units introduces a great deal of uncertainty into statistical estimation. By contrast, measures that are deployed across a larger number of zones (or other comparable units of analysis) are better candidates for evaluation. Similarly, border-enforcement measures that are applied across the entire border and across categories of migrants all at once are not good candidates for such analysis. As a result, not every border-enforcement measure can be assessed using such methods as DID and SCMs.

The limitations created by data requirements and assumptions mean that, even when analysis is feasible, no single statistical method is likely to produce an unbiased and precise estimate of the effects of any border-enforcement measure. In most cases,

---

1 GAO, 2017a, pp. 44–45. Nonetheless, as we suggest in the next section, these data can be analyzed to some extent in follow-up analyses.

2 As the OIG observes, data quality has been "an ongoing issue," with data being "often unreliable and incomplete and statistics are sometimes subject to misinterpretation" (OIG, *CBP's Border Security Efforts: An Analysis of Southwest Border Security Between the Ports of Entry*, Washington, D.C., OIG-17-39, February 27, 2017, p. 13).

therefore, the sensitivity of results obtained from any one method and any single specification of a model must be tested to the extent possible. This might well lead to inconsistent and inconclusive findings. However, this limitation also points to a promising aspect of statistical analysis: Where multiple methods and sensitivity testing produce the same results, one can be more confident in the conclusions.

The Promise and Possibilities of Quasi-Experimental Methods

Notwithstanding limitations, statistical methods of causal inference remain a promising way toward estimating the contributions that various border-enforcement measures make to border security. We highlight two major potential uses of the kind of analysis undertaken here: (1) the potential to come to more-confident and broader-reaching conclusions about the impact and effectiveness of surveillance technology specifically and (2) the potential to use similar approaches to evaluate other border-enforcement measures.

The Potential for More-Confident and Broader-Reaching Conclusions About the Impact and Effectiveness of Surveillance Technology

The analysis detailed in this report was necessarily limited in scope because of data availability and project resources. However, extending this analysis by incorporating additional information and data can produce more-confident conclusions and shed light on the differential effects of different technologies that this study suggests. Our scope was limited to apprehensions, in no small part because of the superior quality and availability of those data. However, investigating the relationship between surveillance asset deployment and other metrics could improve the understanding of the contributions of that technology, to the extent that other metrics are reliably and consistently measured. For example, to further understand the deterrent effects of a technology, examining how the numbers of turn backs are affected by deployments, especially in the initial months, could be informative. Likewise, examining the numbers of got aways could further illuminate the extent to which situational awareness is enhanced. Of course, such an analysis would have to accommodate the previously noted limitations of the data on got aways and turn backs.[3]

Considering and examining other outcomes could shed light on border-crossers' *adaptations* to increased surveillance at the southwestern border. For example, qualitative evidence suggests that migrants are circumventing newly surveilled areas and moving through nearby unsurveilled areas. Investigating whether and to what extent such a displacement effect occurs is important for planning the deployment of resources

---

[3] Although CBP officials assessed that these data were not sufficiently reliable for cross-sector comparisons, comparing zones within sectors might be sufficiently reliable (GAO, 2017a, pp. 44–45). These metrics could thus be used in a sector-specific statistical model akin to the ones we estimate in this study.

where they are needed. An investigation of the effects that surveillance asset deployment has on migrant traffic around the detection radius would require data beyond those employed here. Notably, this would need to take into account natural features of the landscape that shape the most-efficient ways to circumvent surveillance (e.g., terrain, vegetation), as well as data on which zones host other surveillance technology that were not analyzed here.

Similarly, accounts suggest that migrants change other aspects of their crossing behavior, such as group size, preferring to send a larger number of smaller groups rather than a single large group. For instance, a senior CBP official described the change in group size as an adaptation aimed at making it more difficult for the same number of border patrol agents to apprehend large numbers of migrants, whose detection is facilitated by surveillance.[4] Examining patterns in group size could shed light on whether such adaptations are, in fact, systematically taking place; whether they are a response to some technologies but not others; and whether they are seen in some parts of the border but not others. This would require an evaluation of whether such information is consistently available within CBP's database.

Further, acquiring richer information about the context into which new technologies are deployed could shed light on the variable effects that different technologies appear to have. Greater surveillance capabilities would enhance Border Patrol agents' interdiction activities only if agents are deployed where and when they can act on information provided by surveillance. Data on how and where personnel are deployed in connection with new surveillance assets would be crucial in modeling the interaction of these two resources. The effects of surveillance technology are also likely dependent on other conditions in the areas where they are located. Surveillance assets are intended to be integrated into a network of other assets where they are deployed. They might have the greatest impact on some outcomes where sensors and communication technologies are most effectively networked. Information on the integration of newly deployed assets with other technology could illuminate how impact is conditioned by such factors.

Additionally, or alternatively, surveillance assets might have the greatest impact in areas without other technologies to provide domain awareness. For example, our analysis could not incorporate data on unattended ground sensors because information pertaining to the zones (or geographic coordinates) and month of deployment was not available to us. Likewise, data on mobile assets are (understandably) more difficult to obtain than data on fixed assets. If such information can be made available, systematically incorporating data on the preexisting surveillance capabilities into the analysis would be possible.

---

[4] Interview, Washington, D.C., October 23, 2019. For example, large groups of migrants have reportedly become less frequent in Tucson, where IFTs are deployed. See, for example, Rafael Carranza, "Large Groups of Migrants Stop Crossing at the Arizona–Mexico Border," *azcentral*, August 19, 2019.

The Potential for Analysis of Effects of Other Border-Enforcement Measures

In this section, we note the potential for an analysis similar to this one to produce useful results for such measures as other technologies, tactical infrastructure, personnel, and consequences imposed on those crossing the border unlawfully. In theory, quasi-experimental methods, such as DID and SCMs, can be employed to understand the effects of other border-enforcement measures, subject to the limitations noted above. In practice, what would make such analysis possible and useful is improvements to data quality, availability, and integration.

Improvements to data quality, to borrow GAO's description, are efforts to make data "reasonably free from error and bias" and to report data that are "complete, accurate, and timely."[5] Indeed, DHS has made efforts to improve the consistency and quality of some of its data, including data collected at the level of individual migrants (such as the data on apprehensions used here) and data collected on border-enforcement measures, such as technology.[6] These efforts extend to systematizing data that were previously uneven; as noted above, since 2014, the Border Patrol has been mandated to enter certain data that have not been systematically required in the past (i.e., data on "asset assists" and turn backs and got aways).[7] The mandates to enter new data were accompanied by guidance that enables a uniform approach to data recording, the absence of which makes data, such as the pre-2014 turn back and got away measures, not well suited for statistical analysis.[8] Doubtless, further improvements in this direction will enlarge the possibilities for informative analysis using quasi-experimental methods. DHS has also placed an emphasis on improving consistency and transparency of its data.[9] Moreover, steps toward addressing the metrics problem, and producing estimates of outcomes at the border beyond observable data, might also improve the capability of quasi-experimental statistical methods to address the causality problem more generally, beyond surveillance technologies.[10]

Alongside improvements in data quality, data would need to be made available for analysis. This pertains in particular to data on border-enforcement measures themselves. The experience of this study team's efforts to gather data for analysis demonstrated that a variety of actors in DHS maintain the relevant data, making the data difficult to access and synthesize.

---

5 GAO, 2019a, p. 14.

6 See, for example, GAO, 2019a, and DHS, 2019.

7 DHS, 2019, p. 9; GAO, 2018, p. 7.

8 GAO, 2019a, p. 14. GAO lists examples of processes that DHS has employed to improve data quality, including "issuing guidance and monitoring implementation" and "supervisory reviews of data entries."

9 See, for example, GAO, 2019a, and DHS, 2019.

10 For an assessment of DHS efforts to estimate such metrics, see GAO, 2019a.

Related to availability is the integration of what are now disparate data streams and collection processes, which would significantly expand the possibilities for tackling the causality problem. DHS is currently making progress on the immigration data integration initiative, which promises a unified person-centric data set on people as they move through the various parts of the immigration-enforcement system. These improvements, if made available for analysis, could aid future modeling efforts. Modeling of the effects of border-enforcement measures would also be improved with a similar data integration initiative aimed at bringing together data on all border-enforcement measures in an accessible format. The ability to know what kind of resources are deployed, processes followed, operations conducted, and policies adopted at a given time in a given section of the border (e.g., station or zone) would enhance the possibilities for causal inference. In other words, analyses like the one reported here would produce more-confident, -consistent, and -unbiased results if analysts can incorporate the multiple inputs that make up the totality of the U.S. border-enforcement toolbox.

Concluding Observations: Implications for the Department of Homeland Security

In this initial investigation into the impacts of surveillance technology, we found evidence that such impacts are likely uneven across these assets, although the strength of the evidence varies across different technologies. In particular, our analysis suggests that, after the deployment of IFTs, the likely deterrent effect on migrant crossings through surveilled areas overwhelms any boost to situational awareness (or to the capability to detect and apprehend more migrants). By contrast, TASs—and potentially other technologies—might have less of a pronounced deterrent effect and deliver more of a boost to situational awareness. The finding of a deterrent effect is important, in light of the previously observed correlation between multiple changes to border enforcement since 2016 and rising apprehension levels since 2017.[11] Our analysis shows that, notwithstanding such correlation at the national level, more–finely grained analysis still discerns deterrent effects of some border-enforcement measures. Of course, further analysis would be needed to determine the extent to which this deterrent effect is due to merely displacing flows to unsurveilled areas.

As we noted at the outset, the substantive conclusions to be drawn from this study are somewhat limited by our use of apprehensions, in the absence of better solutions to the metrics problem. Although we have shown how the analysis of apprehension levels can be informative, fundamentally, thus-far-unavailable and less ambiguous indica-

11 This has prompted several prominent experts on migration policy to conclude that the "rapid succession of increasingly punitive measures" since 2016 "has had the opposite of the intended effect": "Instead of deterring flows, these measures seem to have signaled . . . that now is the time to migrate, lest conditions continue to become even more difficult" (Capps et al., 2019, p. 7).

tors would be needed to separately identify the effects on situational awareness and deterrence. Yet, further analysis, incorporating other existing data sources as suggested earlier, can support or undermine the findings that are supported by weaker evidence here, as well as shed light on what factors are responsible for these apparently different effects of different technologies. Understanding these effects would put DHS, and CBP in particular, in a better position to understand which surveillance assets would be most appropriate in which settings and conditions.

Between legislative demands, executive policy, and public pressure, the imperative to demonstrate the contributions that different border-enforcement measures make to DHS missions has become more acute in recent years. To do so rigorously, DHS will have to consider solutions to the causality problem, alongside its efforts to grapple with the metrics problem. Beyond satisfying legal mandates, results of quasi-experimental statistical evidence can be combined with other kinds of evidence about the contributions that various border-enforcement measures make to DHS missions in order to inform several decision points. Notably, such analyses can help:

- **Inform decisions about investments into technology and infrastructure.** Significant investments have been and will continue to be made in surveillance technologies and infrastructure along the southwest border. Better evidence about the effects of specific technology or infrastructure could usefully inform a cost–benefit analysis for future investments in similar resources. Since at least the 1993 Sandia National Laboratories study on southwest border security, investments and planned investments into technology and infrastructure—such as those undertaken as part of the Secure Border Initiative—have been plagued by doubts about whether their benefits justify their costs.[12] Analysis that can quantify at least some of the benefits would shed light on these concerns.
- **Inform operational decisions about the deployment of various resources and assets.** The nonuniform results about surveillance technology suggest that various contextual factors shape the ultimate effects of technology assets. The same is likely true of infrastructure, such as fencing or checkpoints. For example, as noted above, where and how CBP personnel are deployed in connection with new surveillance assets quite possibly shapes those assets' ultimate impact on situational awareness and deterrence. Applying quasi-experimental methods that advance understanding of the conditions under which resources are most effective could help operational commanders make decisions about the most-effective patterns of deployments.
- **Inform operational planning and policy responses to migrants' adaptations to the deployment of various resources and assets.** This analysis only began to explore migrant responses to the deployment of surveillance technology, with the

---

12 See, for example, OIG, 2017, pp. 10–13.

results suggesting only that migrants do seek to avoid certain surveillance assets. As we observed, this and other adaptations can be investigated with more data, in response not only to technology but to the deployment of other resources and adoption of policies. Identifying and understanding patterns of adaptations, such as changes in routes or changes in group size, could help planners anticipate and respond to the effects of planned uses of resources.

CBP, like DHS as a whole, has expressed a commitment to incorporating better "quality data and analysis" to inform its operations, investments, and policies, as well as to measuring the extent to which its operations, investments, and policies advance its missions.[13] The kind of analysis conducted here, especially when joined with further improvements to data quality and availability, can contribute meaningfully to these goals.

---

[13] CBP, 2019a, pp. 19, 23.

APPENDIX

Technical Details

The Difference-in-Differences Analysis

Models for a Single Treatment

Our DID models are implemented using a negative binomial regression specification: The outcome is assumed to obey a negative binomial distribution, and its mean on the log scale is modeled as a function of fixed effects for the respective time period (in months) and zone in addition to a treatment status indicator. Specifically, the mean function for a model that incorporates a single technology (i.e., treatment) is given by

$$\log\left(\mu_{jt}\right) = \beta_t + \gamma_j + \alpha D_{jt}, \qquad \text{A.1}$$

where μ_{jt} is the expected outcome value for zone j at month t; β_t is a fixed effect for month t; γ_j is a fixed effect for zone j; α is the technology's effect; and D_{jt} is an binary indicator variable equaling 1 if zone j is treated by the technology at month t and is 0 otherwise. Note that this model does not contain covariates that can predict the outcome. These are excluded here because none of the available covariates varies over time, and time-invariant covariates would be absorbed by the zone-level fixed effects.

Model A.1 can be modified to incorporate a nonbinary treatment status. Let

$$\log\left(\mu_{jt}\right) = \beta_t + \gamma_j + \alpha R_{jt}, \qquad \text{A.2}$$

where R_{jt} is the continuous treatment measure, which, in our case, gives the portion of zone j covered by the technology's prespecified radius at month t.

We report the effect of treatment as a percentage change, which is calculated as $\delta = 100 \times \left[\exp(\alpha) - 1\right]$. That is, for Model A.1, δ denotes the percentage change in expected outcome that would have been observed if a zone that was untreated at month t had instead been considered treated at that time. For Model A.2, δ denotes the percentage change in outcome that would have been observed if a zone that was 0-percent treated at month t had instead been 100-percent treated at that time.

Models for Multiple Treatments

Models A.1 and A.2 can be extended to simultaneously evaluate multiple technologies. Specifically, for four technologies (IFT, TAS, RAID towers, and RVSS), we let

$$\log(\mu_{jt}) = \beta_t + \gamma_j + \alpha_1 D_{1jt} + \alpha_2 D_{2jt} + \alpha_3 D_{3jt} + \alpha_4 D_{4jt}, \tag{A.3}$$

where, for $\ell = 1,\dots,4$, α_ℓ is the effect of technology ℓ, and $D_{\ell jt}$ is an indicator variable equaling 1 if zone j is treated by the technology ℓ at month t and is 0 otherwise. Note that $D_{\ell jt}$ can be replaced by nonbinary treatment measure $R_{\ell jt}$ to create an analogue of Model A.2. Additionally, we used $\delta_\ell = 100 \times [\exp(\alpha_\ell) - 1]$ for $\ell = 1,\dots,4$ as our estimator of the treatment effect.

Models with Sector-Level Trends

We next extend those models to account for annual trends in outcome at the sector level in addition to the baseline levels of the outcome as quantified at the zone level.[1] In this vein, we alter the notation so that index i indicates the sector and index j indicates zones within sectors. Furthermore, consider

$$\log(\mu_{jt}) = \beta_t + \gamma_{ij} + \omega_{is} + \alpha_1 D_{1ijt} + \alpha_2 D_{2ijt} + \alpha_3 D_{3ijt} + \alpha_4 D_{4ijt}, \tag{A.4}$$

where γ_{ij} is a fixed effect for zone j (in sector i) and ω_{is} is a fixed effect for sector i at calendar year s (where time t occurs in year s). That is, this model allows (annual) trends in outcome at the sector level that are in addition to those captured by the other fixed effects and the treatment indicators. Like with Model A.2, $D_{\ell jt}$ in Model A.3 can be replaced by nonbinary treatment measure $R_{\ell jt}$ to create an analogue of Model A.2.

All DID models are fitted using the glm.nb() function in the R package MASS.[2] Among other things, this function returns point estimates, standard errors, and p-values for the treatment effect coefficients. We recognize that the specified models likely understate uncertainty.[3] For this reason, more-robust procedures for evaluating

---

[1] We note that, if area-specific trends were included at the zone level, the estimated effect of treatment would likely be consequentially reduced.

[2] W. N. Venables and B. D. Ripley, *Modern Applied Statistics with S*, 4th ed., New York: Springer, 2002.

[3] There are several explanations for this phenomenon. First, DID regression specifications require parametric assumptions regarding the behavior of the data that, if not satisfied, will complicate efforts to quantify uncertainty. In addition, the approaches commonly used to approximate uncertainty assume homogeneity, in that, after regression predictors are taken into account, the outcomes are independent across time and space. However, homogeneity might not hold, and unmeasured spatial or temporal correlation in outcomes could be expected. See, for example, Coady Wing, Kosali Simon, and Ricardo A. Bello-Gomez, "Designing Difference in Difference Studies: Best Practices for Public Health Policy Research," *Annual Review of Public Health*, Vol. 39, April 2018, pp. 461–462.

uncertainty, such as bootstrapping and permutation methods for DID models, are advisable in future efforts to use these data to identify the effects of border-enforcement measures.

In the next section, we report the point estimates and *p*-values for the main sets of models relied on here.

Results

Models described as "separate" include each technology separately in a single regression; models described as "joint" include all specified technologies in a single regression. Each outcome—that is, total apprehensions, apprehensions of Central American migrants, and apprehensions of Mexican migrants—is analyzed separately.

Table A.1
Difference-in-Differences Regression Results, Basic Models, Separate

	Estimated Effect			
Apprehensions	**IFT**	**TAS**	**RAID Tower**	**RVSS**
Total	–44.0***	3.0	–24.1***	–7.8**
Central American migrants	–64.3***	–14.3*	–45.7***	–19.9***
Mexican migrants	–30.0***	4.8	0.0	–25.6***

NOTE: Results for IFT and TAS are based on the analysis of 573 zones over 68 months; results for RAID, of 573 zones over 62 months; and results for RVSS, of 573 zones over 76 months. *** = $p \leq 0.01$. ** = $p \leq 0.5$. * = $p \leq 0.1$.

Table A.2
Difference-in-Differences Regression Results, Basic Models, Joint

	Estimated Effect			
Apprehensions	**IFT**	**TAS**	**RAID Tower**	**RVSS**
Total	–49.2***	–8.6	–19.3***	3.6
Central American migrants	–67.1***	–14.5*	–42.9***	–4.7
Mexican migrants	–31.2***	–11.9**	5.4	–20.8***

NOTE: Results are based on the analysis of 573 zones over 76 months. *** = $p \leq 0.01$. ** = $p \leq 0.5$. * = $p \leq 0.1$.

Table A.3
Difference-in-Differences Regression Results, Divergent-Trends Models, Joint

	Estimated Effect			
Apprehensions	**IFT**	**TAS**	**RAID Tower**	**RVSS**
Total	–26.5***	26.6***	27.0***	34.8***
Central American migrants	–56.0***	64.8***	17.8	11.5*
Mexican migrants	–8.5*	7.2	52.6***	6.5

NOTE: Results are based on the analysis of 573 zones over 76 months. *** = $p \leq 0.01$. ** = $p \leq 0.5$. * = $p \leq 0.1$.

Table A.4
Difference-in-Differences Regression Results, Divergent-Trends Models, Separate

	Estimated Effect			
Apprehensions	**IFT**	**TAS**	**RAID Tower**	**RVSS**
Total	–23.9***	25.9***	34.8***	31.8***
Central American migrants	–56.5***	55.1***	27.2**	6.8
Mexican migrants	–8.8*	16.1***	60.6***	6.0

NOTE: Results for IFT and TAS are based on the analysis of 573 zones over 68 months; results for RAID, of 573 zones over 62 months; and results for RVSS, of 573 zones over 76 months. *** = $p \leq 0.01$. ** = $p \leq 0.5$. * = $p \leq 0.1$.

Table A.5
Difference-in-Differences Regression Results, Sector-Specific Models

	Estimated Effect		
Apprehensions	**IFT**	**TAS**	**RAID Tower**
Total	–20.5***	31.7***	35.4***
Central American migrants	–55.5***	54.1***	28.7***
Mexican migrants	–7.9*	23.0***	62.9***

NOTE: Results for IFT are based on the analysis of 63 zones and 68 months; results for TAS, of 58 zones and 68 months; and results for RAID, of 58 zones and 62 months. *** = $p \leq 0.01$. ** = $p \leq 0.5$. * = $p \leq 0.1$.

Synthetic Control Methods

As an alternative to the DID models, we consider SCMs, which require a different formulation and some less restrictive assumptions. Building on the classic setting of

Alberto Abadie and his colleagues, we considered a method by Robbins, Saunders, and Kilmer designed for disaggregated data in which multiple cases collectively compose the treated area.[4] One limitation of SCMs in our setting is that they require that the treatment (i.e., technology) to be implemented at a single point in time. The phased rollout of the technologies considered here violates this requirement. To address this issue, we segment the rollout of each technology into groups, in which, for each group, the respective technology is assumed to have been implemented at a single point in time (i.e., the respective group was subject to one phase of the rollout of the technology). We then use synthetic controls to evaluate the effect of each phase of the rollout individually.

SCMs involve the development of a synthetic control, which is a weighted combination of untreated zones. Each untreated zone is assigned a nonnegative weight (however, in the evaluation of any given phase of the rollout of a technology, we dropped zones that previously received the technology from inclusion in the set of potential synthetic controls).

Weights were selected to satisfy three sets of constraints. For notation purposes, we assumed that there were J_0 and $J - J_0$ pre- and postintervention zones, respectively, and T_0 and $T - T_0$ pre- and postintervention time periods (in months), respectively. Specifically, letting w_j denote the nonnegative weight assigned to (untreated) zone j, we imposed first

$$\sum_{j=1}^{J_0} w_j = J_0 - J,$$

such that weights summed to the number of treated zones. Likewise, letting $\mathbf{R}_j$ indicate a vector of time-invariant covariates for zone j, we imposed

$$\sum_{j=1}^{J_0} w_j \mathbf{R}_j = \sum_{j=J_{0+1}}^{J} \mathbf{R}_j,$$

such that the synthetic control matched the treated zone across all covariates. Letting Y_{ijt} indicate the value of outcome i in zone j at time t, we enforced

$$\sum_{j=1}^{J_0} w_j Y_{kjt} = \sum_{j=J_{0+1}}^{J} Y_{kjt}$$

[4] Alberto Abadie and Javier Gardeazabal, "The Economic Costs of Conflict: A Case Study of the Basque Country," *American Economic Review*, Vol. 93, No. 1, March 2003, pp. 113–132; Abadie, Diamond, and Hainmueller, 2010; Robbins, Saunders, and Kilmer, 2017.

for each outcome k and each preintervention time t for $1 \le t \le T_0$. These constraints ensured that the synthetic control maximally matched the treated zones across outcomes and covariates across all preintervention time points.

After finding a satisfactory set of weights w_j for each untreated case j, we used the term

$$\sum_{j=1}^{J_0} w_j Y_{kjt}$$

for $t > T_0$ to estimate the cumulative value of outcome i that would have been observed in each zone in the absence of the surveillance asset. We therefore estimated the effect of the asset deployment on outcome i, aggregated across all postintervention times, as follows:

$$\hat{\alpha}_k = \sum_{t=T_0+1}^{T} \left(\sum_{j=J_0+1}^{J} Y_{kjt} - \sum_{j=1}^{J_0} w_j Y_{kjt} \right).$$

Effects were calculated as percentage change from the counterfactual:

$$\frac{100\hat{\alpha}_i}{\sum_{t=T_0+1}^{T} \sum_{j=1}^{J_0} w_j Y_{kjt}}.$$

If outcomes are modeled jointly, this generates a single set of weights incorporating all outcome constraints but reports separate estimates for each outcome.

This approach is implemented with the microsynth package in R.[5] If microsynth cannot identify nonnegative weights w_j that exactly satisfy each constraint, a quadratic programming method finds nonnegative weights that satisfy constraints as closely as possible. Uncertainty is modeled with a permutation approach with 1,000 permutation groups.

Results

SCM results for the analysis of the five analytic deployment areas of IFTs are shown in Tables A.6 through A.10. Furthermore, results for the two analytic deployment areas of TASs are given in Tables A.11 and A.12, whereas results for the five analytic deployment areas of RAID are shown in Tables A.13 through A.17. Results for the five deployment areas of RVSSs are in Tables A.18 through A.22.

Columns in the tables indicate the cumulative number of postdeployment months incorporated in order to produce the respective treatment effect estimate. Blank entries indicate that there was not enough postdeployment data to produce the

---

[5] Robbins and Davenport, 2019.

Table A.6
Synthetic Control Method Results for Integrated Fixed Tower Deployment in Region 1: Five Zones in August 2015

	Estimated Effect				
Apprehensions	6 Months	12 Months	18 Months	24 Months	36 Months
Total	−23.2***	−26.2**	−36.1**	−36.0***	−39.6***
Mexican migrants	12.1	9.3	2.4	1.2	−1.4
Non-Mexican migrants	−33.9***	−32.3**	−39.1**	−38.5**	−39.8**

NOTE: Each column heading indicates the cumulative number of postdeployment months incorporated in order to produce the respective treatment effect estimate. For the first IFT deployment region, matching is poorer for subcategories of total apprehensions (both Mexican and non-Mexican), so results could be subject to bias; matching is also less close for total apprehensions than it is for subsequent deployments of IFTs but not as poor as for subcategories of the total. *** = $p \leq 0.01$. ** = $p \leq 0.5$.

Table A.7
Synthetic Control Method Results for Integrated Fixed Tower Deployment in Region 2: Seven Zones in April 2017

	Estimated Effect				
Apprehensions	6 Months	12 Months	18 Months	24 Months	36 Months
Total	15.9	−12.6	−24.7*	−37.9*	
Mexican migrants	−7.7	−31.8***	−36.9***	−49.4***	
Non-Mexican migrants	−18.5*	−39.3**	−44.9**	−55.8**	

NOTE: Each column heading indicates the cumulative number of postdeployment months incorporated in order to produce the respective treatment effect estimate. A blank cell indicates that there was not enough postdeployment data to produce the respective cumulative estimate. *** = $p \leq 0.01$. ** = $p \leq 0.5$. * = $p \leq 0.1$.

Table A.8
Synthetic Control Method Results for Integrated Fixed Tower Deployment in Region 3: Six Zones in October 2017

	Estimated Effect				
Apprehensions	6 Months	12 Months	18 Months	24 Months	36 Months
Total	−41.1	−44.0	−47.0		
Mexican migrants	−35.5*	−32.4*	−24.9		
Non-Mexican migrants	−32.1	−34.9	−36.4		

NOTE: Each column heading indicates the cumulative number of postdeployment months incorporated in order to produce the respective treatment effect estimate. A blank cell indicates that there was not enough postdeployment data to produce the respective cumulative estimate. * = $p \leq 0.1$.

Table A.9
Synthetic Control Method Results for Integrated Fixed Tower Deployment in Region 4: Five Zones in September 2018

	Estimated Effect				
Apprehensions	**6 Months**	**12 Months**	**18 Months**	**24 Months**	**36 Months**
Total	–26.4				
Mexican migrants	–11.7				
Non-Mexican migrants	–31.9*				

NOTE: Each column heading indicates the cumulative number of postdeployment months incorporated in order to produce the respective treatment effect estimate. A blank cell indicates that there was not enough postdeployment data to produce the respective cumulative estimate. * = $p \leq 0.1$.

Table A.10
Synthetic Control Method Results for Integrated Fixed Tower Deployment in Region 5: Four Zones in December 2018

	Estimated Effect				
Apprehensions	**6 months**	**12 months**	**18 months**	**24 months**	**36 months**
Total	–58.9**				
Mexican migrants	10.9				
Non-Mexican migrants	–62.5**				

NOTE: Each column heading indicates the cumulative number of postdeployment months incorporated in order to produce the respective treatment effect estimate. A blank cell indicates that there was not enough postdeployment data to produce the respective cumulative estimate. ** = $p \leq 0.5$.

Table A.11
Synthetic Control Method Results for Tactical Aerostat System Deployment in Region 1: Six Zones in January 2014

	Estimated Effect				
Apprehensions	**6 Months**	**12 Months**	**18 Months**	**24 Months**	**36 Months**
Total	54.0	77.1***	100.4***	120.3***	136.9***
Mexican migrants	51.0**	68.4***	84.3***	91.9***	82.2***
Non-Mexican migrants	64.5	81.8**	104.3***	140.4***	206.3***

NOTE: Each column heading indicates the cumulative number of postdeployment months incorporated in order to produce the respective treatment effect estimate. *** = $p \leq 0.01$. ** = $p \leq 0.5$.

respective cumulative estimate. For all analyses of total apprehensions (regardless of technology being studied), synthetic control weights were calculated by matching the zones' respective deployment area to control zones across three years of quarterly total

Table A.12
Synthetic Control Method Results for Tactical Aerostat System Deployment in Region 2: Ten Zones in August 2015

	Estimated Effect				
Apprehensions	**6 Months**	**12 Months**	**18 Months**	**24 Months**	**36 Months**
Total	−6.3	−7.8	−11.7	−13.3	−18.3
Mexican migrants	−14.7	−12.5	−8.8	−9.8	−15.1
Non-Mexican migrants	−10.0	−13.1	−24.4	−25.6	−30.9

NOTE: Each column heading indicates the cumulative number of postdeployment months incorporated in order to produce the respective treatment effect estimate. For the second TAS deployment, matching is poor, so results could be subject to bias.

Table A.13
Synthetic Control Method Results for Rapid Aerostat Initial Deployment Tower Deployment in Region 1: Two Zones in October 2015

	Estimated Effect				
Apprehensions	**6 Months**	**12 Months**	**18 Months**	**24 Months**	**36 Months**
Total	3.0	4.0	11.9	14.8	38.9
Mexican migrants	58.4	59.5	60.5	58.0	65.1
Non-Mexican migrants	−11.2***	−10.6**	−1.3	2.7	33.0

NOTE: Each column heading indicates the cumulative number of postdeployment months incorporated in order to produce the respective treatment effect estimate. For the first RAID tower deployment, matching is poor for the Mexican subcategory, so results could be subject to bias. *** = $p \leq 0.01$. ** = $p \leq 0.5$.

Table A.14
Synthetic Control Method Results for Rapid Aerostat Initial Deployment Tower Deployment in Region 2: Two Zones in November 2015

	Estimated Effect				
Apprehensions	**6 Months**	**12 Months**	**18 Months**	**24 Months**	**36 Months**
Total	−15.3*	−26.9*	−34.0**	−34.2**	−41.3**
Mexican migrants	5.6	0.6	−1.8	−0.5	2.9
Non-Mexican migrants	−48.9**	−54.5**	−56.5**	−57.3**	−59.8**

NOTE: Each column heading indicates the cumulative number of postdeployment months incorporated in order to produce the respective treatment effect estimate. ** = $p \leq 0.5$. * = $p \leq 0.1$.

apprehension counts (in the time immediately prior to the respective deployment) and five zone-level, time-invariant covariates (median income, unemployment, population,

Table A.15
Synthetic Control Method Results for Rapid Aerostat Initial Deployment Tower Deployment in Region 3: Two Zones in May 2016

	Estimated Effect				
Apprehensions	**6 Months**	**12 Months**	**18 Months**	**24 Months**	**36 Months**
Total	–4.5**	4.4	–0.2	–3.4*	
Mexican migrants	12.8	20.2	18.7	17.9	
Non-Mexican migrants	–22.5***	–8.4**	–7.7**	–6.8**	

NOTE: Each column heading indicates the cumulative number of postdeployment months incorporated in order to produce the respective treatment effect estimate. A blank cell indicates that there was not enough postdeployment data to produce the respective cumulative estimate. For the third RAID tower deployment, matching is poor for the non-Mexican subcategory, so results could be subject to bias.
*** = $p \leq 0.01$. ** = $p \leq 0.5$. * = $p \leq 0.1$.

Table A.16
Synthetic Control Method Results for Rapid Aerostat Initial Deployment Tower Deployment in Region 4: One Zone in September 2016

	Estimated Effect				
Apprehensions	**6 Months**	**12 Months**	**18 Months**	**24 Months**	**36 Months**
Total	–40.6***	–39.1***	–38.5***	–37.5***	
Mexican migrants	25.4	12.9	4.8	6.5	
Non-Mexican migrants	–43.6***	–42.9***	–41.7***	–40.3***	

NOTE: Each column heading indicates the cumulative number of postdeployment months incorporated in order to produce the respective treatment effect estimate. A blank cell indicates that there was not enough postdeployment data to produce the respective cumulative estimate. For the fourth RAID tower deployment, matching is poor for all subcategories, so results could be subject to bias.
*** = $p \leq 0.01$.

area in square miles, and whether the zone touches the border).[6] For all analyses of apprehension counts for Mexican and non-Mexican migrants, weights were created by matching across the same five covariates, as well as three years of predeployment quarterly apprehension counts for Mexican migrants and three years of predeployment quarterly apprehension counts for non-Mexican migrants simultaneously. In certain cases, synthetic control matching was poor, which might imply bias in the estimates of treatment effects. Such cases are noted in the tables.

[6] These data were obtained from recent iterations of the ACS and matched to Border Patrol zones. ACS data at the census tract level were used. Interpolation was performed to split tracts that overlapped multiple zones.

Table A.17
Synthetic Control Method Results for Rapid Aerostat Initial Deployment Tower Deployment in Region 5: One Zone in December 2017

	Estimated Effect				
Apprehensions	**6 Months**	**12 Months**	**18 Months**	**24 Months**	**36 Months**
Total	−27.0**	−34.0**			
Mexican migrants	53.8	46.5			
Non-Mexican migrants	−48.2***	−54.0**			

NOTE: Each column heading indicates the cumulative number of postdeployment months incorporated in order to produce the respective treatment effect estimate. A blank cell indicates that there was not enough postdeployment data to produce the respective cumulative estimate. For the fifth RAID tower deployment, matching is poor for all subcategories, so results could be subject to bias. *** = $p \leq 0.01$. ** = $p \leq 0.5$.

Table A.18
Synthetic Control Method Results for Remote Video Surveillance System Deployment in Region 1: Three Zones in December 2014

	Estimated Effect				
Apprehensions	**6 Months**	**12 Months**	**18 Months**	**24 Months**	**36 Months**
Total	39.0	34.3	14.9	−5.2	−8.7
Mexican migrants	123.4	144.1**	146.4***	151.3***	137.4***
Non-Mexican migrants	−29.5	−13.3	−28.3	−29.0	−42.3***

NOTE: Each column heading indicates the cumulative number of postdeployment months incorporated in order to produce the respective treatment effect estimate. For the first RVSS deployment, matching is poor for all subcategories, so results could be subject to bias. *** = $p \leq 0.01$. ** = $p \leq 0.5$.

Table A.19
Synthetic Control Method Results for Remote Video Surveillance System Deployment in Region 2: 14 Zones in January 2016

	Estimated Effect				
Apprehensions	**6 Months**	**12 Months**	**18 Months**	**24 Months**	**36 Months**
Total	−33.1	−39.0*	−40.6**	−42.4***	−51.8***
Mexican migrants	−18.3	−4.6	−9.5	−11.2	−13.7
Non-Mexican migrants	−53.1	−61.3**	−65.2***	−72.7***	−77.9***

NOTE: Each column heading indicates the cumulative number of postdeployment months incorporated in order to produce the respective treatment effect estimate. For the second RVSS deployment, matching is poor for all subcategories, so results could be subject to bias. *** = $p \leq 0.01$. ** = $p \leq 0.5$. * = $p \leq 0.1$.

Table A.20
Synthetic Control Method Results for Remote Video Surveillance System Deployment in Region 3: 11 Zones in August 2016

	Estimated Effect				
Apprehensions	**6 Months**	**12 Months**	**18 Months**	**24 Months**	**36 Months**
Total	70.5	58.1	98.9*	139.1***	
Mexican migrants	–20.6	–21.9	–41.6*	–44.4**	
Non-Mexican migrants	72.3	49.2	89.0*	121.8***	

NOTE: Each column heading indicates the cumulative number of postdeployment months incorporated in order to produce the respective treatment effect estimate. A blank cell indicates that there was not enough postdeployment data to produce the respective cumulative estimate. For the third RVSS deployment, matching is poor for all subcategories, so results could be subject to bias. *** = $p \leq 0.01$. ** = $p \leq 0.5$. * = $p \leq 0.1$.

Table A.21
Synthetic Control Method Results for Remote Video Surveillance System Deployment in Region 4: Six Zones in January 2018

	Estimated Effect				
Apprehensions	**6 Months**	**12 Months**	**18 Months**	**24 Months**	**36 Months**
Total	226.0**	243.0***			
Mexican migrants	43.6**	20.5			
Non-Mexican migrants	324.0**	357.3***			

NOTE: Each column heading indicates the cumulative number of postdeployment months incorporated in order to produce the respective treatment effect estimate. A blank cell indicates that there was not enough postdeployment data to produce the respective cumulative estimate. For the fourth RVSS deployment, matching is poor for all subcategories, so results could be subject to bias. *** = $p \leq 0.01$. ** = $p \leq 0.5$.

Table A.22
Synthetic Control Method Results for Remote Video Surveillance System Deployment in Region 5: Four Zones in August 2018

	Estimated Effect				
Apprehensions	**6 Months**	**12 Months**	**18 Months**	**24 Months**	**36 Months**
Total	49.9				
Mexican migrants	–45.9***				
Non-Mexican migrants	94.8				

NOTE: Each column heading indicates the cumulative number of postdeployment months incorporated in order to produce the respective treatment effect estimate. A blank cell indicates that there was not enough postdeployment data to produce the respective cumulative estimate. For the fifth RVSS deployment, matching is poor for all subcategories, so results could be subject to bias. *** = $p \leq 0.01$.

Bibliography

Abadie, Alberto, Alexis Diamond, and Jens Hainmueller, "Synthetic Control Methods for Comparative Case Studies: Estimating the Effect of California's Tobacco Control Program," *Journal of the American Statistical Association*, Vol. 105, No. 490, June 2010, pp. 493–505.

———, "Comparative Politics and the Synthetic Control Method," *American Journal of Political Science*, Vol. 59, No. 2, April 2015, pp. 495–510.

Abadie, Alberto, and Javier Gardeazabal, "The Economic Costs of Conflict: A Case Study of the Basque Country," *American Economic Review*, Vol. 93, No. 1, March 2003, pp. 113–132.

Angrist, Joshua David, and Jörn-Steffen Pischke, *Mostly Harmless Econometrics: An Empiricist's Companion*, Princeton, N.J.: Princeton University Press, 2008.

Arizona Public Media, "Tucson Sector Border Patrol Chief on Trends Along Southern Border," September 13, 2019. As of November 7, 2019:
https://news.azpm.org/p/news-topical-border/2019/9/13/
158142-border-patrol-chief-on-trends-along-southern-border/

Bailey, John W., Sarah K. Burns, David F. Eisler, Clare C. Fletcher, Thomas P. Frazier, Brandon R. Gould, Kristen M. Guerrera, Terry C. Heuring, Brian Q. Rieksts, Bryan Roberts, and John E. Whitley, "Assessing Southern Border Security," Institute for Defense Analyses, Paper NS P-5304, May 2016.

Capps, Randy, Doris Meissner, Ariel G. Ruiz Soto, Jessica Bolter, and Sarah Pierce, *From Control to Crisis: Changing Trends and Policies Reshaping U.S.–Mexico Border Enforcement*, Washington, D.C.: Migration Policy Institute, August 2019. As of November 7, 2019:
https://www.migrationpolicy.org/sites/default/files/publications/
BorderSecurity-ControltoCrisis-Report-Final.pdf

Carranza, Rafael, "Large Groups of Migrants Stop Crossing at the Arizona–Mexico Border," *azcentral*, August 19, 2019.

CBP—*See* U.S. Customs and Border Protection.

Chang, J., S. Calkins, D. McGarvey, N. Kallfa, L. Nguyen, M. Roberts-Lahti, and P. Keller, Homeland Security Studies and Analysis Institute, *Strategic Sampling Framework for Surveillance Mission Needs Analysis*, prepared for U.S. Customs and Border Protection, U.S. Department of Homeland Security, Homeland Security Studies and Analysis Institute Report RP 14-14-03, 2016, Not available to the general public.

DHS—*See* U.S. Department of Homeland Security.

Espenshade, Thomas J., "Using INS Border Apprehension Data to Measure the Flow of Undocumented Migrants Crossing the U.S.–Mexico Frontier," *International Migration Review*, Vol. 29, No. 2, Summer 1995, pp. 545–565.

GAO—*See* U.S. Government Accountability Office.

Gramlich, John, and Luis Noe-Bustamante, "What's Happening at the U.S.–Mexico Border in 5 Charts," *Fact Tank*, November 1, 2019. As of November 11, 2019: https://www.pewresearch.org/fact-tank/2019/11/01/whats-happening-at-the-u-s-mexico-border-in-5-charts/

Kreif, Noémi, Richard Grieve, Dominik Hangartner, Alex James Turner, Silviya Nikolova, and Matt Sutton, "Examination of the Synthetic Control Method for Evaluating Health Policies with Multiple Treated Units," *Health Economics*, Vol. 25, No. 12, December 2016, pp. 1514–1528.

Long, Dave, "CBP's Eyes in the Sky: CBP's Tethered Aerostats Keep Watch for Trouble from 10,000 Feet," U.S. Customs and Border Protection, undated. As of November 7, 2019: https://www.cbp.gov/frontline/frontline-november-aerostats

Marosi, Richard, "Towers and Cameras, Not a Wall, Keep Migrants from Crossing the Border into Arizona," *Los Angeles Times*, April 16, 2018. As of November 7, 2019: https://www.latimes.com/local/california/la-me-border-tech-20180416-story.html

Morral, Andrew R., Henry H. Willis, and Peter Brownell, *Measuring Illegal Border Crossing Between Ports of Entry: An Assessment of Four Promising Methods*, Santa Monica, Calif.: RAND Corporation, OP-328-OSD, 2011. As of December 8, 2019: https://www.rand.org/pubs/occasional_papers/OP328.html

Office of Immigration Statistics, U.S. Department of Homeland Security, *Efforts by DHS to Estimate Southwest Border Security Between Ports of Entry*, September 2017. As of November 7, 2019: https://www.dhs.gov/sites/default/files/publications/17_0914_estimates-of-border-security.pdf

Office of Inspector General, U.S. Department of Homeland Security, *CBP's Border Security Efforts: An Analysis of Southwest Border Security Between the Ports of Entry*, Washington, D.C., OIG-17-39, February 27, 2017. As of November 7, 2019: https://www.oig.dhs.gov/sites/default/files/assets/2017/OIG-17-39-Feb17.pdf

OIG—*See* Office of Inspector General.

Public Law 107-296, Homeland Security Act of 2002, November 25, 2002. As of May 12, 2019: https://www.govinfo.gov/app/details/PLAW-107publ296

Public Law 114-328, National Defense Authorization Act for Fiscal Year 2017, December 23, 2016. As of December 8, 2019: https://www.govinfo.gov/app/details/PLAW-114publ328

Public Law 115-31, Consolidated Appropriations Act, 2017, May 5, 2017. As of December 8, 2019: https://www.govinfo.gov/app/details/PLAW-115publ31

Robbins, Michael W., and S. Davenport, "Microsynth: Synthetic Control Methods for Disaggregated and Micro-Level Data in R," *Journal of Statistical Software*, preprint, 2019.

Robbins, Michael W., Jessica Saunders, and Beau Kilmer, "A Framework for Synthetic Control Methods with High-Dimensional, Micro-Level Data: Evaluating a Neighborhood-Specific Crime Intervention," *Journal of the American Statistical Association*, Vol. 112, No. 517, 2017, pp. 109–126.

Roberts, Bryan, *Measuring the Metrics: Grading the Government on Immigration Enforcement*, Washington, D.C.: Bipartisan Policy Center, February 19, 2015. As of November 7, 2019: https://bipartisanpolicy.org/report/measuring-the-metrics-grading-the-government-on-immigration-enforcement/

Rosenblum, Marc R., and Faye Hipsman, *Border Metrics: How to Effectively Measure Border Security and Immigration Control*, Migration Policy Institute, January 2016. As of November 7, 2019:
https://www.migrationpolicy.org/research/border-metrics-how-effectively-measure-border-security-and-immigration-control

U.S. Border Patrol, "United States Border Patrol: Nationwide Illegal Alien Apprehensions Fiscal Years 1925–2018," c. March 2019. As of November 7, 2019:
https://www.cbp.gov/sites/default/files/assets/documents/2019-Mar/bp-total-apps-fy1925-fy2018.pdf

U.S. Census Bureau, "American Community Survey (ACS)," homepage, undated. As of November 18, 2019:
https://www.census.gov/programs-surveys/acs

U.S. Code, Title 6, Domestic Security; Chapter 1, Homeland Security Organization; Subchapter III, Science and Technology in Support of Homeland Security; Section 185, Federally Funded Research and Development Centers. As of May 12, 2019:
https://www.govinfo.gov/app/details/USCODE-2017-title6/USCODE-2017-title6-chap1-subchapIII-sec185

U.S. Customs and Border Protection, U.S. Department of Homeland Security, "Integrated Fixed Towers Certified," March 22, 2016. As of November 8, 2019:
https://www.cbp.gov/newsroom/national-media-release/integrated-fixed-towers-certified

———, *Strategy 2020–2025*, Publication 0883-0419, April 2019a. As of November 7, 2019:
https://www.cbp.gov/sites/default/files/assets/documents/2019-Jun/CBP-2020-2025-Strategy-Plan-Document-FINAL-508-compressed.pdf

———, "231 Central Americans Surrender to Tucson Sector Border Patrol," media release, April 30, 2019b. As of November 7, 2019:
https://www.cbp.gov/newsroom/local-media-release/231-central-americans-surrender-tucson-sector-border-patrol

U.S. Department of Homeland Security, *Department of Homeland Security Border Security Metrics Report*, February 26, 2019. As of November 7, 2019:
https://www.dhs.gov/sites/default/files/publications/ndaa_border_metrics_report_fy_2018_0_0.pdf

U.S. Government Accountability Office, *Border Security: DHS Surveillance Technology, Unmanned Aerial Systems and Other Assets*, Washington, D.C., GAO-16-671T, May 24, 2016. As of November 7, 2019:
https://www.gao.gov/products/GAO-16-671T

———, *Southwest Border Security: Additional Actions Needed to Better Assess Fencing's Contributions to Operations and Provide Guidance for Identifying Capability Gaps*, Washington, D.C., GAO-17-331, February 2017a. As of November 7, 2019:
https://www.gao.gov/products/GAO-17-331

———, *Southwest Border Security: Border Patrol Is Deploying Surveillance Technologies but Needs to Improve Data Quality and Assess Effectiveness*, Washington, D.C., GAO-18-119, November 2017b. As of November 7, 2019:
https://www.gao.gov/products/GAO-18-119

———, *Border Security: Progress and Challenges with the Use of Technology, Tactical Infrastructure, and Personnel to Secure the Southwest Border*, Washington, D.C., GAO-18-397T, March 15, 2018. As of November 7, 2019:
https://www.gao.gov/products/GAO-18-397T

———, *Border Security: DHS Should Improve the Quality of Unlawful Border Entry Information and Other Metric Reporting*, Washington, D.C., GAO-19-305, March 21, 2019a. As of November 7, 2019: https://www.gao.gov/products/GAO-19-305

———, *Border Security: Assessment of the Department of Homeland Security's Border Security Improvement Plan*, Washington, D.C., GAO-19-538R, July 16, 2019b. As of November 7, 2019: https://www.gao.gov/products/GAO-19-538R

Venables, W. N., and B. D. Ripley, *Modern Applied Statistics with S*, 4th ed., New York: Springer, 2002.

Wing, Coady, Kosali Simon, and Ricardo A. Bello-Gomez, "Designing Difference in Difference Studies: Best Practices for Public Health Policy Research," *Annual Review of Public Health*, Vol. 39, April 2018, pp. 453–469.